THE HOUSE OF ABUSE

Understanding Violence in the Home

MICHAEL F. McGRANE

THE HOUSE OF ABUSE
Understanding Violence
in the Home

To Gayle,
my soul and inspiration.
She has made me the person I am today.

To our children,
Kindra, Patrick, and Kelsey,
who always thought I was in the CIA because I never
talked about my work. I hope they will read this book
so they can finally know what I did every day.

CONTENTS

INTRODUCTION

A twelve-year-old boy stands behind the door in his bedroom, his two younger brothers cowering at his side. He has his baseball bat in hand while waiting in the dark.

On the other side of the door, his father is drunk and screaming at his mother. He is threatening to kill her and the boys. The oldest brother stands afraid, yet ready to defend his mother and brothers. The night finally goes quiet as his father passes out on the living room couch. Once again, they survived another day.

Twenty years later, the oldest brother, now thirty-two years old, is court-ordered to a counseling group for men who have abused their partners.

It is reported that one in four women and men in America has been or will be a victim of domestic violence (National Coalition Against Domestic Violence, 2017; Centers for Disease Control and Prevention). This statistic is difficult to research because violence in the home is often not reported. Violent acts in private spaces may never become known, yet their impact on the victims is devastating.

Domestic abuse is a *crime*. Far too often it goes unreported or the seriousness of this "private" or "personal" matter is played down, considered best left to the individuals involved. After thirty-plus years of working face-to-face with perpetrators and victims/survivors of domestic abuse, I know this crime can have an extremely damaging and long-term impact on people's lives.

Some people die from domestic assaults, but most will live. The lives of the victims will never be the same. There are no winners. Everybody loses. But there *are* survivors, and it is *their* stories that we need to hear.

Very few people will have the opportunity to do what I have done in my career. There are many occupations where thousands of people are trained to provide specific kinds of services, such as teachers, nurses, lawyers, plumbers, auto mechanics, and others. By comparison, relatively few people will facilitate counseling groups for perpetrators or victims of domestic violence. From this unique viewpoint I describe what happens behind the closed doors in a treatment group for men who have been abusive in their intimate partner relationships. I also address some of the women's perspectives and experiences.

When writing this book, I became aware of how much information a person can accumulate in thirty-plus years of work. I realized I couldn't possibly write about all I have learned and experienced. Therefore, my goal is to provide a sample of the things I recall as being significant. Although it will be an incomplete list, I will tell some of the stories of my journey to help men end abuse in *The House*.

CHAPTER ONE

The Journey Begins

I have been thinking about writing this book for a very long time. I developed the exercise *The House of Abuse* in 1981 when I was director of Violence Prevention and Intervention Services (VPIS). Since that time, several authors have reproduced it in their books. Therapists have used this tool in their counseling sessions with perpetrators and victims/survivors of domestic abuse.

As founder and director, I spent countless hours in counseling groups and designing various programs with our staff. The VPIS program described in the following pages was one of the largest and most comprehensive domestic abuse counseling programs in the country and became nationally and internationally known and replicated. The staff provided counseling and support services for thousands of perpetrators and victims/survivors over three decades. Men, women, children, and adolescents were served in multiple settings to address the impact that violence played in these individuals' lives.

The House exercise was developed to help men who had been abusive in their intimate partner relationships. Its purpose is to define and discuss the types of abuse that happen in each room. It is a basic exercise to identify the types of abuse that occur in a home and provide a way for these men to recognize and acknowledge their abusive behaviors.

This exercise has also been used in victims/survivors' groups with women who have been abused. It has been a powerful exercise for perpetrators and victims/survivors of domestic abuse because it captures the types of abuse that have occurred and their impact on people's lives.

The House exercise has been implemented in professional trainings and with general audiences throughout the United States and abroad. It has been adopted in other settings, such as the military's domestic abuse programs, chemical dependency treatment, law schools, college classrooms, and churches.

This book explores in great detail *The House* and the stories that happen within. It focuses on the men who perpetrate abuse against their intimate partners, but it addresses the victims/survivors of the abuse and their issues and stories as well. Related topics such as couples counseling, therapists' roles, and alcohol and drug abuse are also discussed in these pages.

My purpose in writing this book is to increase awareness of what domestic abuse is by sharing my firsthand experiences with this issue. And, while my hope is that everyone who plans to be involved in an intimate relationship at some point in their life will read this book, I do aim to reach a few groups in particular.

First, my ultimate hope is that women who have been or are victims/survivors of intimate partner abuse will find this book. Women who have previewed this book have said things like, "I guess I was more abused than I ever thought." Many reported that they had become numb or desensitized to the abuse and accepted it as part of their relationships. After reading this book, however, women could readily identify the abuse they endured. The stories gave them insight into the men's thinking and behaviors.

Second, I hope that young women who are in dating relationships will read this book. A checklist in chapter 8 poses questions that can help identify signs of an unhealthy abusive relationship (see page 118). Men in dating relationships should also look for the signs of an unhealthy relationship. The questions provide information on what to look for in a partner's behavior. Women who have read this book recalled their past dating relationships and the signs of abuse that went unnoticed. A common response is they thought he would change, or that they could change him.

Women who participated in the victims/survivors' groups described in these pages gained critical insight into and knowledge of their victimization from abuse. As a result, many made dramatic changes in their lives, claiming that if they had this knowledge sooner, their pasts would have been totally different. Hopefully, readers will relate to the women's experiences told in this book and find the courage to seek support.

The next group I hope to reach includes clinicians, social workers, therapists, psychologists, victim advocates, chemical dependency counselors, teachers, nurses, doctors, clergy, police, and others who have contact with victims and perpetrators of domestic violence. Those who work with children and youth should also find this book to be helpful.

I also hope that men who are non-abusive in their relationships will read this book to gain a better understanding of the issue of domestic abuse. Fathers with daughters and sons who are in dating relationships may benefit from this information. This book would also be useful to men who have been abusive in their relationships. I know this audience will be difficult to reach.

More broadly, the general public is an audience for this

book. We all need to know what goes on "behind closed doors" in *The House*. It is my goal that the reader will attain a deeper awareness and understanding of abuse in *The House*. This abuse has been misunderstood and hidden from view for far too long. One out of four of us has been or will be victims of domestic violence. And *all of us*, whether we realize it or not, know someone who is a victim or perpetrator of domestic abuse. It could be a friend, a family member, a neighbor, a teacher, or a church member. *You* could be the one to offer support or uncover the "secret" of domestic abuse in someone's life.

An Epidemic of Domestic Violence

In recent years public awareness about domestic violence has increased. Stories about celebrities, sports stars, and other famous people have been featured in the news media, on television, and in movies.

Additional training on this issue is available for counselors, medical professionals, educators, clergy, the police, and the courts. Warning signs, causes, and effects are being studied at colleges and even in high schools. Yet the issue is still one that puzzles most of us.

People often ask me: "Why do women stay in abusive relationships?" "Why don't they just leave?" Or "Do these men who abuse women ever really change?" Often this line of questioning is followed by a comment: "I wouldn't put up with it." Or "They should lock them up and throw away the key!" These questions and comments will be addressed in chapter 8.

Another frequent question is "What about women who abuse?" Men in the counseling groups are always quick to ask this one. The answer is yes: women can also abuse. Anyone can be abusive. Men, women, children, and adolescents all can be perpetrators or victims of abuse. I address this issue in chapters 8 and 11.

Domestic violence has been around for as long as humans have been in relationships. There has yet to be a public outcry to address this problem. Over recent decades, several groups, mostly women's groups, have tried to draw needed attention to this issue. Their tireless efforts have yielded some progress.

If 25 percent of the population in this country is experiencing a life-threatening disease, it is considered an epidemic. According to the research, we have an epidemic of domestic violence on our hands. The sad truth is that a public outcry to address this problem will probably never happen.

I wish I could be more optimistic about the potential for ending domestic violence in our homes. But many people are working every day with victims and perpetrators of domestic abuse to help them end the violence in their lives. We need more people to help with this effort. We all have a part to play. Reading this book may help you discover your part.

"Normal Violence"

When giving a talk on the topic of domestic abuse, I often ask the audience: What is "normal violence"? It is a strange question. People's answers are as diverse as the attendees themselves.

I break it down a bit by asking the audience what movies or television shows they remember watching as a child that were the most violent. Naturally, the answers are often determined by when you were born. Baby boomers of the late '40s through the mid-'60s would give one answer. It might be the flying monkeys in *The Wizard of Oz*, or maybe the crocodile in the original *Peter Pan*. Millennials would give a totally different set of answers. It might be something by Stephen King or "slasher" movies. Move forward to the next generation and the responses were once again different.

You can probably already guess what happens when we compare the answers. With each generation, the movies and television shows were increasingly more violent. My parents, who grew up in the 1920s, couldn't believe what was on television and in movies in the '60s. Today, many would argue that the violence displayed on televisions, in video games, and in theaters has desensitized us to how violent our society has become.

But the question is "What is normal violence?" Our own answers will give us some insight into how we view what is normal or even "acceptable violence." For far too long, violence in the home has been tolerated or seen as acceptable by many. *The House* provides a look at what happens to one out of four of us in our homes today.

Throughout the book I use words such as *domestic abuse, domestic violence,* or *family violence.* While it can be argued that these terms have different meanings or implications, for the sake of brevity they are interchangeable in this writing.

Also, titles like *counselors, therapists, clinicians,* and *facilitators* are used interchangeably. Although the credentials of these individuals vary, the descriptions refer to persons providing counseling, support, or therapy to program participants.

The word *perpetrator* is used to describe the men and women who have been abusive toward their intimate partners or children. I also describe victims of domestic abuse as *survivors.*

Over the past decades, many different program models and treatment approaches have been developed to serve men and women in abusive relationships. Throughout the book, I describe some of my experiences working with the men, women, children, and adolescents who participated in our program. I do not claim to have the "right" or "only" way of addressing this complex issue. However, my three decades of working directly with perpetrators and victims/survivors has provided me with a firsthand look at what happens in *The House*.

CHAPTER 2

Startup

This chapter briefly addresses background topics: program philosophies, characteristics of the men, the intake process, and the structure of the group treatment model.

Not Total Agreement

During the 1980s and '90s, various treatment programs for men were developed using different models and philosophies. Like other businesses, programs became competitive and some claimed their approach was the "best."

Nobody had the "cure" or "right answer" to ending men's violence against women. I told our staff they should draw the best material from all of the programs. We never claimed to have the right or only way to address men's violence. We had what we believed to be an effective treatment approach. We continued to learn and develop better ways by constantly adapting our treatment methods.

Not everyone who has worked with men who have abused their intimate partners will agree with all of these interventions and treatment strategies. Some may not agree with my conclusions in chapter 12. And others who have been facilitating men's groups for a long time will have their own treatment approaches.

Who Were the Men?

The program was located in an inner-city neighborhood. The majority of the group participants were white or African American. Some men from other ethnic groups were also referred. A culturally sensitive/specific African American group and a Hmong men's group were later designed and implemented (see chapter 11). A Spanish-speaking men's group was also developed by a collaborative agency and housed in the program.

There are gay and transgender men who are abusive in their intimate relationships. There are also men who have been abused by their intimate partners. It was our practice to refer these men to appropriate resources and programs. The men's perpetrator groups were not a safe place for gay or transgender men. The male victims/survivors needed a different treatment model than the one offered by our men's program.

Ninety-nine percent of the men served by our program were court-ordered to the groups. Typically, the men had been charged with a misdemeanor for domestic assault. In most cases this involved a sentence of one year probation and up to ninety days in jail or the county workhouse. Some of the men had previously been involved in the courts for a variety of offenses. A few had long juvenile criminal records, while others were first-time adult offenders. I estimate that more than 70 percent of the men had alcohol or drug issues. Most were poor, and many were without jobs. The majority had poor reading and writing skills, and some could not read or write.

The Intake

For several reasons, there were two options for intake to the program.

The first option involved three to four individual sessions with each man prior to the group. The counselor who would be facilitating the group conducted these sessions. The counselor collected a detailed assessment of each man's criminal and mental health history and chemical use. The men completed an extensive questionnaire about the abuse toward their partners and children. These individual intake sessions served several purposes. In addition to gathering important information, they provided an opportunity to build a relationship with the men. The sessions also prepared them for what was to come in the treatment group. Many of these appointments were "no shows" that took up valuable staff time. This option became a major issue regarding the best use of staff resources. The hours spent conducting intakes for each of the men attending the groups posed serious budget and staffing problems. However, an important benefit of this option was it provided an early indicator of how likely the man was to complete the program.

A second intake option did not require individual sessions prior to the group. Instead, the men were told when the group would start and they would be required to show up on the first night.

PROS AND CONS

Most counselors preferred to provide individual sessions with the men prior to the group. The advantages of this option far outweighed its disadvantages as the counselors collected histories and established a therapeutic relationship. Screening out men who did not show up for the individual sessions helped to determine who would attend the group.

The second option, where no intake sessions were offered prior to the group, produced some interesting first night group experiences. Picture twelve to fifteen court-ordered men waiting in a lobby for the group to start. They didn't know the counselor or the other men sitting next to them. They had no idea what was to happen next. Plus, they were angry and didn't want to be there. In this scenario, there was an increased chance the men would be more aggressive and challenging toward the counselor. This situation was not ideal.

Over the years I experienced both of these options. If there was an advantage to the second option, it was that the men didn't know what was coming next. Sitting with other men whom they did not know kept them uncomfortable and silent for the most part. Occasionally men started talking about their displeasure at being there and began colluding with each other to form a negative alliance. This instant connection added to the challenge of conducting a positive start for the group.

The Group Structure

The group sessions were two and a half hours in length. The group met once a week for sixteen weeks. The variations of groups offered are described in appendix 1.

Many of the groups had a solo facilitator. If there was a co-facilitator the role of each would be determined beforehand. This understanding was critical because it established both facilitators as equal and in sync with each other. Cofacilitation is addressed in appendix 1.

Men Don't Talk

Some men had previously been in a counseling group. Typically, it would have been an alcohol or drug treatment program. But for most of them, this was their first time in treatment. A counseling group can be a very foreign and uncomfortable experience—and often it seems to be even more threatening for men. Bar or garage talk was something familiar and comfortable for them. Typical subjects included cars, sports, women, and other "manly" topics. It was safe to say none of the men had talked seriously with other men about their relationship issues. No one had talked about the abuse they had perpetrated against their partners. Many uncomfortable discussions would be required throughout the sixteen-week group experience. It was not going to be a "good old boys" club.

CHAPTER THREE

Before Building

This chapter briefly addresses what needs to be discussed prior to building *The House* in the men's groups.

The Four Foundation Statements

One concept that is essential to cover before building *The House* is that of the Four Foundation Statements. These will be referred to throughout the group treatment.

1. I am responsible for my own behavior
2. Provocation does not justify violence
3. The 100 percent rule (not two to tango or 50–50)
4. The only person I can control is myself

It's important to establish the Four Foundation Statements as true and agreed upon, at least by the majority of the men. These statements generate much discussion and are not an easy sell. They provide the foundation for the first step in taking responsibility for one's own behavior. The Four Foundation Statements are explained more fully in chapter 4.

Setting the Stage for The House:
Night One of the Group

You can probably imagine that men who are court-ordered to attend a counseling group for domestic assault are not exactly thrilled about being there. This is an understatement.

Remember the opening story of the twelve-year-old boy standing ready to save his mother's and brothers' lives? He is now sitting in a circle with other men who have abused their intimate partners. He, as well as some of the others, now has children who are hiding from him. A judge has sentenced these men for a criminal charge of domestic assault. Their sentences are stayed with the condition that they successfully complete a domestic abuse treatment program. They are also assigned to one year or more of probation and must meet all conditions set forth by the courts.

In the Ring

Try to picture this circle of ten to fifteen men. Put yourself in that circle as the counselor. Your job is to help men who believe they don't need help. The men's body language tells it all. They look angry; they are verbally hostile, throwing out questions and negative comments. You know they aren't going to like the answers you give them.

This scenario reminds me somewhat of a lion tamer at the circus: he is the only one in the ring, surrounded by not-so-friendly or -cooperative lions. I held no whip, but the men viewed me as someone with power over them. Still, this knowledge didn't stop them from chewing on me if they got the chance. My goal, just like the lion tamer's, was to take charge, but also to de-escalate the situation as quickly and respectfully as possible.

Building trust in an extremely distrustful group of angry

men was not easy to do. However, establishing trusting relationships is essential to the group process. Anyone who works with humans knows that it's all about relationships.

What the Men Believe

One of my initial statements to the group is "No one deserves to be abused." This statement would seem hard to argue against, yet many of the men would defend themselves by saying, "she deserved it!" Men often felt they were "victims" of abuse by their partners. My response was, "If that is true, you need to make some decisions about your relationship." These decisions might involve leaving and ending the relationship. They could involve seeking some additional counseling. But these decisions were for another time and place. This time would be spent on ending their abuse and hopefully making a better life for themselves and others.

Establishing a "partial" agreement on the Four Foundation Statements helps to prepare the men for what will come next. This first group exercise gets the men talking about their perspectives and beliefs. It also acknowledges their anger and resentment about being ordered to attend the group. Finally, it confronts the men's alleged abuse by their partners. The next chapter covers the first group session in great detail, describing more interventions made prior to the second group session, where the participants build *The House*.

CHAPTER FOUR

First Group Session

This chapter provides a detailed account of a first session for a men's group, prior to the men building *The House* in session two. It is told in the first person, describing some of my experiences in these groups.

There is no exact or predictable description of what could happen—everything from a total mutiny to a very rare, semi-cooperative experience is possible. First group sessions challenge even the most skilled clinician.

The main goal of the first session is to set the tone and agenda for what is to come. The first hour is highly critical in terms of establishing guidelines and building a trusting relationship with the men. Here my role felt much more like that of the lion tamer I referred to earlier. Every first group session involved resistance from the participants. Indeed, on a resistance scale of 1–10, most groups were initially at a 15.

Group Introductions

First, I introduced myself by my first name. Then I asked the men to give their first names. I thanked them for coming to the group and acknowledged they already had taken a big first step. I let them know other men chose not to come to the group and, unfortunately, they would suffer the consequences. I understood they didn't want to be in the group. Most claimed the "system" was unfair and they didn't have a problem with abuse. I told them I was aware of their feelings and had heard most of these concerns before. I pointed out I wasn't there when their incident occurred. I didn't know the facts about what did or did not happen, and I never would.

It's Your Choice

I started by telling the men they had two options. They could choose to stay and participate in the group, or they could go back to court and talk with the judge. Most of the men did not see attending the group versus going to jail as much of a choice. I reminded them that those who didn't show for the group had already made their choice. I knew they wanted to tell me their side of the story. I told them they would get their chance to speak, but first I wanted to say a few things.

Next I said, "In jail, you can sit and do your time. In fact, it may be easier. However, if you choose to stay in this group, it is not about doing time. The expectation is you will participate and abide by the things required to complete the program." This statement brought about loud grumblings and verbal outbursts. It was a juggling act trying to listen to their comments yet maintain order. Many years of experiencing this part of beginning a group helped me know this too would pass. Over decades, the faces changed, but the comments and hostility remained the same.

Claimed Innocence

The vast majority of the men were court-ordered to attend the group. Virtually all claimed they were innocent of the charges. Hopefully, by the end of the sixteen weeks, some would acknowledge they in fact were not as innocent as they initially proclaimed.

Open Parachute

After addressing some of the men's comments and concerns, I told a story. It started with a question: "Has anyone ever jumped out of an airplane?" Most of the time the answer was no. However, a few veterans and skydivers in the groups would say yes.

I acknowledged I had never jumped out of a perfectly good airplane and didn't plan to do so. But I had heard from skydivers that it was an unbelievable rush. They reported you could look around and take in an incredible view. I also recognized that the veterans who had jumped with an enemy shooting at them had a very different experience. I asked, "What would happen if you pulled the cord and your parachute failed to open? What would you be thinking? Would you still be enjoying the view? Most likely, you would be thinking about the sudden stop at the end. Right?"

Most of the men had come to the group with a closed mind. I'd tell the group, "Our mind is like a parachute: it only works when it is open. My job and the job of all of us in the group is to help each other keep our minds/parachutes open. We need to help each other when we see someone's parachute starting to close. Remember: we know the end result of a closed chute." I told the men that the one thing I would ask them to do during the time they were in the group was to keep their parachutes open. I emphasized it was not just the counselor's job but also the group's job to help each other keep their chutes open.

A Lifetime of Trauma

I told the men something they weren't expecting to hear. If they were like the thousands of other men I worked with in these groups, they had experienced enough trauma and abuse to last them a lifetime. This statement always caught them off guard. I explained that, almost without exception, men in these groups had been victims of abuse in their own homes as young boys or young men. Either they had experienced the abuse directly or they watched as it was perpetrated on someone they loved. I stated I was not there to shame, punish, or rub their noses in what they had done. Even though most of the men viewed the group as punishment, I asked them to try to view it as help. I explained that I knew they didn't know what was to come in the weeks ahead, but I asked them to give it a chance and try to work together to help each other complete the program.

PTSD in The House

The mental health diagnosis of post-traumatic stress disorder (PTSD) is commonly associated with combat veterans experiencing war trauma. It has also been a diagnosis for victims/survivors of domestic abuse.

In the earlier years of the men's groups there were veterans from the war in Vietnam. Later years included veterans from the wars in the Middle East. Many had not sought out counseling for the symptoms associated with their war experiences. I encouraged the veterans to seek help and offered to connect them with resources that would address their needs. The men's domestic abuse groups were not an appropriate place to deal with these issues.

I talked about the trauma that affected victims in *The*

House. Like in wars, there are hidden scars that last a lifetime and often go unrecognized or discussed. One difference between the traumas that happened in war versus the trauma that happens in an abusive home is that in war there is an identified enemy; in the home, there is no "enemy." The home is supposed to be a safe place where people are loved and cared for.

Hopefully, someday the victims of violence in *The House* will gain an increased public awareness like our combat veterans plagued by war trauma. We need to provide the same compassion, understanding, and support to the victims of family violence that we are finally beginning to offer our combat veterans. Unfortunately, in most cases, the support and help does not come until it's too late. The children in these homes go unnoticed and become adults who are suffering from the consequences of their pasts.

The Promise

At this point in the group I spoke about the "promise."

With few exceptions, men who witnessed or experienced abuse as children made a familiar promise to themselves. I asked the group, "What was the promise?" Almost without fail someone answered, "I will never do that to my wife or kids." Other group members would nod in agreement. The men knew the promise. At that moment, several of the men would begin to open their chutes.

Bad Deal

I exclaimed how sad and angry it made me feel knowing so many children had experienced abuse in their lives. Children in violent homes were dealt a bad hand of cards. I continued, "Sadly, this trauma for most of you has never been addressed." I let them know the past couldn't be changed and it couldn't be used as an excuse. We can only change what we do in the present and the future. They would be responsible for what "cards" they dealt now.

I made it clear we would spend only a brief amount of time in this group talking about the abuse they experienced in their childhoods. They would need to reach out for more help to deal with some of those issues. I offered them an option to meet with me privately or I could provide other counseling resources for them. Unfortunately, most would never seek additional help.

Opening the door to let the men know they likely had been victims of abuse was a bit of a slippery slope. The men would quickly jump to the alleged abuse they felt their partners had done to them. I let them know we would not spend time talking about how they think their partners had abused them. Their partners were not here. We would only be dealing with "our" abuse, not the alleged abuse from their partners.

Predicting How Many Will Change

I asked, "How many men out of a hundred do you think will actually change their abusive behaviors and live violence-free lives?" Their answers were pretty interesting. Most gave a very low number. I then asked, "How many men in this group do you think will make the change to end their abusive behaviors?" This question had become more personal, and they sometimes were reluctant to guess. I pushed them for an answer, but I kept in mind that these men were not yet ready to accept they had a problem with abuse.

Your Turn to Talk

It was now their turn to talk. However, the subjects I had raised were not what they wanted to talk about. I addressed their comments and resistance but moved them quickly to the next exercise. I reminded them they still had a choice to continue or leave the group.

Introduction Exercise

The next exercise was an effort to break the resistance and get the group members to focus on something other than their anger. Ideally, this activity would be the first step in helping the group start to bond. The exercise involved having pairs of men introduce themselves by first name. Next, they needed to find out one thing the group member liked about himself. The paired men would ask these two questions of each other. Then they would go around the circle and introduce the man they had just met, including the thing he liked about himself.

A GOOD THING

The identified "good thing" men liked about themselves varied. Most would cite a certain job or skill, like being a good mechanic or good at sports. Some would say they were a good father. Others weren't able to come up with anything. Sometimes a member needed help to think of a good thing. I would encourage the group to help the member find a good thing, not letting anyone take a pass. Many men also couldn't remember the person's name they were introducing. It was important the men start calling each other by name. This connection made the experience more personal. They would be required to talk about many personal things later.

Sometimes I would take the exercise one step further and ask, "Who can name everyone in the group?" Someone always volunteered. I might also ask if they could name what each man liked about himself. Again, this activity helped the men focus on each other rather than on their anger and resistance about being in the group.

The Reminder

After this group exercise, it was time to return to the opening message: "Is your parachute open or closed?" I reminded them that the only thing 1 would ask of them was to keep their parachutes/minds open. I warned them it would be tough to do. Some would never open their chutes. I emphasized that this was their group and I was not the only person responsible for checking to see if someone's chute was open or closed. Our goal as a group was to help keep everyone's mind open.

No Guarantee

Change is one of the most difficult things to do, especially when you think you don't have anything to change. There was no guarantee the program would change the men's abusive behaviors. They needed to do it themselves.

I offered a final challenge: "Sadly, very few of you will put forth the effort needed to make real change. If the abusive behavior doesn't end, it's guaranteed things will only get worse." Imprisonment and loss of family or jobs are possible consequences of continued abuse. Serious injury or even death can occur if the abuse doesn't stop. I shared a favorite quote: "You can lead a horse to water, but you can't make him drink." A Catholic priest who was a recovering alcoholic famously finished the quote with "but you can make him damn thirsty!" I told the group, "As I see it, my job is to make you damn thirsty!"

Setting Group Expectations and Rules

It is critical that the group members be involved in setting the expectations and rules for the group. It is also important to put these rules in writing and post them in plain view. It is essential to generate this list in the first group session, as it provides a concrete document to counter any later argument from members who test these rules. If necessary, they could be reviewed before every group meeting.

Setting the expectations for a group was a challenging task. The facilitator always had to know what needed to be on the list. Surprisingly, the participants did an adequate job of generating a basic list, including items such as no drugs or alcohol, respecting others, no violence, being on time for the group, what's said in the group stays in the group, and so on.

It was important that the clinician explain their legal obligation as a therapist to report certain information to the authorities. There is mandatory reporting of child abuse or neglect. If participants revealed abusing a child, the law requires the counselor to report the abuse to Child Protection. Also, if any group members threatened to hurt someone or themselves, the counselor was mandated by law to call the police. In addition, the therapist needed to inform the men what information would be reported to probation officers or the courts.

Other situations needed further clarification, like what would happen if someone was suspected of being under the influence of drugs or alcohol. What did "confidentiality" mean as it applied to the group? What would be the consequence if someone were late or missed group? Other rules included no eating or drinking while in the group. This rule may sound trivial, but when men were eating snacks and opening pop cans, they were not listening to what was being said. Instead, it felt like the men were in their living rooms watching a football game.

Cell phones needed to be turned off during group. Men struggled to comply with this rule, claiming they needed to be contacted in case of an emergency. Often, they tried to peek at their phones or attempted to text. I would use some humor and tell them I had a huge collection of cell phones in my office.

Lastly, men needed to use the restroom prior to group. No restroom breaks would be allowed. If this rule were not put in place, half of the group time would involve men going to the bathroom.

Four Foundation Statements

Next I introduced the Four Foundation Statements. Depending upon how much time was taken in the introductions and rules exercises, these could be presented in the second group session, prior to building *The House*.

The Four Foundation Statements needed to be posted in plain view, along with the list of group rules and expectations.

❶ I am responsible for my own behavior
❷ Provocation does not justify violence
❸ The 100 percent rule
❹ The only person I can control is myself

These statements always generated some interesting and important discussions. Basically, they all say the same thing, but each would bring out different attitudes and perspectives.

1. I AM RESPONSIBLE FOR MY OWN BEHAVIOR

The first statement laid the foundation for the first goal of the program. In order for a person to have any hope of ending their abusive behavior, they need to take full responsibility. It is much like the first step of taking responsibility for one's alcohol or drug abuse. Most of the time the men agreed to the first statement. However, resistance to this concept would show up quickly during discussion of the statements that followed.

2. PROVOCATION DOES NOT JUSTIFY VIOLENCE

The second statement produced the biggest objection from the men. It was the most difficult for them to accept. They continued to blame others for their actions. "What if the other person did this or said this?" Men were not convinced their partner's actions or words didn't provoke their abuse.

3. THE 100 PERCENT RULE

The goal of the 100 percent rule is to put a stop to the old idea "It takes two to tango (or fight)." This thinking implies each person has a part in the argument or fight. It places blame on both parties involved.

Here is the difference with the 100 percent rule. If a partner called you a name, that's 100 percent her problem. If you chose to call your partner a name, that is 100 percent your problem, not 50–50. You can choose not to call a name and, thus, not have a problem.

4. THE ONLY PERSON I CAN CONTROL IS MYSELF

The last Foundation Statement points to the men taking responsibility for their actions. There are multiple ways to control other people, usually by some kind of force. It could be physical force, verbal force, sexual force, or emotional force. But control always involves force.

I would give an example of force to make a point. "Pretend I have a gun pointing at your head. Next, I tell you to go over and open the door. How would you respond?" The men's responses varied from "I'd go open the door" to "Kiss my ass" to the famous "Make my day!" The point was someone could control someone else, but in most cases it would take a threat or act of violence.

These Four Foundation Statements laid the groundwork for men to start taking responsibility for their abuse. I frequently referred back to these statements throughout the sixteen weeks of group.

Blame

An issue that came up throughout the group sessions was the men's constant attempts to blame their partners. I told the group we would not spend time on blaming their partners. I posted a sign in the group room, a circle with the word "BLAME" inside and a line drawn through it. This concept, along with the group rules and expectations and the Four Foundation Statements, was often revisited during the group sessions.

The majority of the men's relationships with their partners were over. The men would say, "I got rid of the problem; it was her, so I don't need to be here." I reminded them that more than likely they would become involved in another intimate relationship in the future. Many had already been in several relationships that failed due to their abuse.

A classic example of blame happened later on when the men built *The House*. They would exclaim that their partners did every one of those things to them! One woman told me her partner brought home a copy of *The House* and told her, "See, this is what you do to me!"

The System Was Unfair

Men frequently argued that the system was "unfair." They might say, "It's a woman's state" or "The deck is stacked against men." The men wanted to know, "What about the women who are abusive?" "Why aren't they being punished and sent to a group?" My reminder to these men was that women who are abusive would need to address their abuse. But they were not in this group. This group was for the men who were here. "Everyone is responsible for his or her own behavior. It's what we all agreed on earlier." The only person I can control is myself.

Pit Bull Ring

Another story I told was about an event that happened in a neighboring county. It received major news coverage. A ring of men was discovered fighting pit bulls just outside the city. Sheriffs surrounded the area, and a helicopter was flown in to aid with the bust. On the ground, there was a major effort by law enforcement to capture the guilty parties. The men involved were charged with felonies or gross misdemeanors for animal cruelty and other offenses. Many were jailed or imprisoned.

WHAT'S FAIR?

I went on: "I consider myself to be an animal lover. I've had pets for most of my life. I don't think animals should be abused. If you think the system that landed you here is unfair, I agree with you. Today, most of you have been charged with a misdemeanor, not a felony." Here's where I made my point: "Do you think it's right that someone who abuses his spouse, girlfriend, or child should be charged with a lesser crime than someone who abuses an animal?

Let's say you had a daughter who was being abused by a boyfriend or husband: would you be satisfied if a system valued her less than if she were a dog?"

MEN'S RESPONSE

The response from the men was not unexpected. They still struggled with the system that sent them to treatment. Some men accepted the story and agreed human beings should not be treated worse than animals. Counselors who facilitate men's groups are constantly confronted by men's logic and attitudes throughout the process. "The system is unfair" argument was one men continued to put forth.

Holding men accountable for their actions was a constant challenge. It required patience and skill on the part of the counselor. The men would continue to blame their partners for their situations. At these times, I would again ask the group: "Are your parachutes open?"

Who Are the Unlucky Ones?

I made a few more final statements regarding the system being unfair. I referred to the statistic that one out of four people would be victims of abuse in their homes. "Right now, there are men abusing their partners and maybe their children in their homes. Tell me, who are the unlucky ones? Is it you guys who are here in this group, who have a chance to get help to end your abuse? Or is it the men who are, right now, abusing their partners or children, creating fear and trauma in their homes?

"Most of you know what it looks like because you grew up in this kind of home. It may be too long ago and you have forgotten some of your feelings. You may have become numb and blocked out those memories.

"The system won't ever be fair. The real question is:

what are you going to do for the next four months we are together? Are you willing to open your parachutes and take an honest look at yourselves? Or will you return to your current homes or future homes and continue in your old ways?

"It's your choice. You alone will decide your own outcome. All the counseling in the world won't change you. You are the only one who can change yourself. If you're not ready or willing to look at your abuse, then don't waste your time and the group's time. You are free to leave now. But if you choose to stay, we have work to do."

The men's initial concerns and feelings had been acknowledged and addressed. The counselor's role had been clarified, and the group's expectations and rules had been established. The men were given a picture of what to expect in the group counseling experience. All of these steps helped them start to trust the process and bond as a group.

Different Strategies

Other clinicians who facilitate these types of men's groups have different treatment strategies and counseling styles. I've described a couple of mine, but, needless to say, I've had to try alternatives if one approach wasn't working. Things sometimes took an unwanted turn and needed to be dealt with differently. It would be easy to get into a power struggle with the men. The ability to hold men accountable yet not back them into a corner took some advanced skill and experience.

One important skill a counselor needs to develop is relationship building. You can imagine how challenging a task this might be, given the makeup of the group. Trust of the counselor is nonexistent at the start. It takes time for the men to view the facilitators as fair and helpful. Some might never accept them as anything other than an authority figure.

These men were very good at escalation. The therapist's ability to de-escalate is critical to prevent any unwanted or potentially dangerous situations from occurring. It requires exceptional skill to hold the men accountable for their abuse in a way that doesn't escalate into a verbal or even potentially physical confrontation. In my years of facilitating mandatory, court-ordered men's groups I never had a physical act of violence occur in a group. There were many intense situations that could easily have gone wrong. These two crucial skills, building trusting relationships and de-escalation, are key to providing a safe and violence-free group experience.

On to the Second Group Session

In the second men's group session I would introduce *The House* exercise. In this session the men's anger and hostility were still present. Many group members were locked into blaming their partners for their situation. They felt falsely accused. Changing their behavior was the furthest thing from their minds. After all, they believed they were innocent. Their only real goal was getting done with the group and not going to jail. However, some men appeared to have mellowed a bit since the first session.

Building *The House* usually would take up the entire second session. The men would be engaged in this exercise, and a great deal of discussion would take place. This exercise set the expectation for the men that they would be required to participate and not sit and "do time."

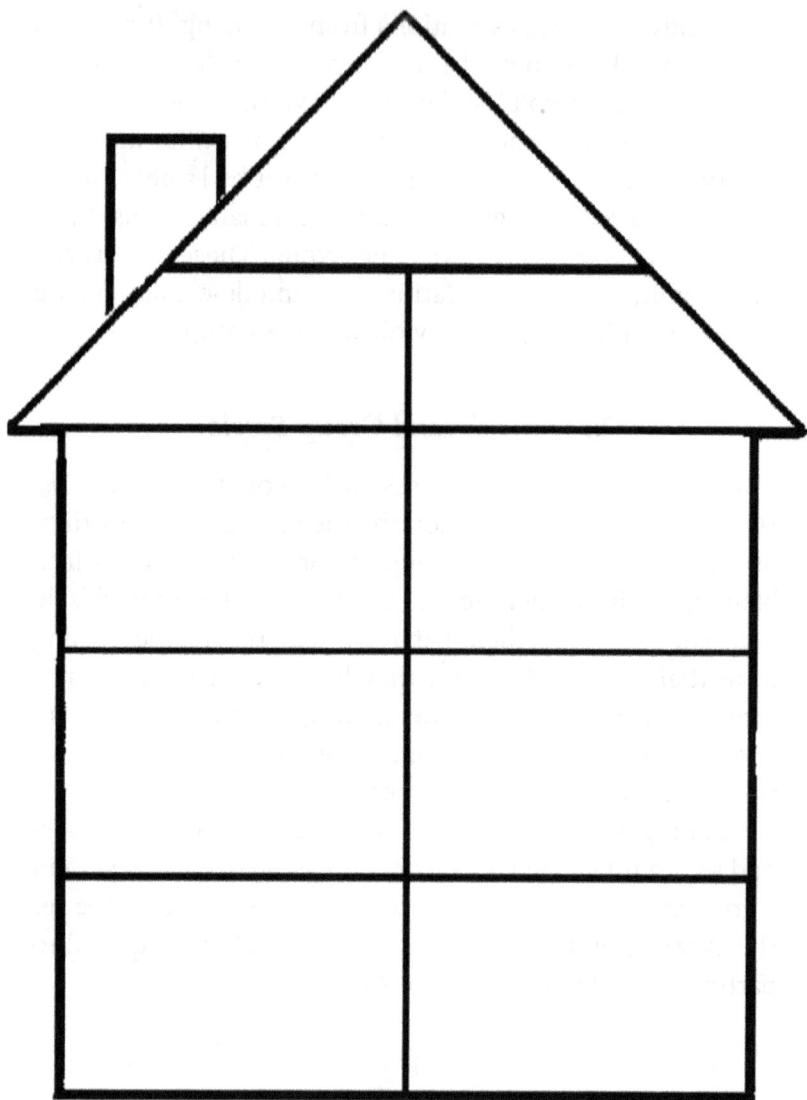

Developed by Michael F. McGrane, 1983

CHAPTER FIVE

The House of Abuse

The group setting has the men sitting in a circle and a picture of a blank *House* with its nine empty rooms displayed on a board or a large poster paper. The participants are asked to fill in the blank rooms (see diagram on opposite page) with the different types of abuse. It is important to let the men "build" *The House*. The task is to help them fill in the rooms with their own words. This exercise typically takes one to two hours to complete.

Some men would not say a word. Some sat with arms crossed or tried to interrupt the process with their comments. It is challenging to address the interruptions while getting men to participate in building *The House*. The exercise can go off the rails in a hurry.

The stories in this section are written from the perspective of men who have been abusive toward their intimate partners. The setting describes what happens in a court-ordered, men's domestic abuse treatment group.

In this chapter, the reader will have the opportunity to "build" *The House*, much like the men did in the group.

The Universal House

When I developed *The House of Abuse,* I was seeking an intervention tool that could be used to help men look at their abusive behaviors. The idea of *The House* came to mind. I later realized it made sense that this image is fairly universal. One person's house could be made of lumber or bricks, while another's house could be made of mud and straw. Yet, when talking about violence in the home, *The House* metaphor seemed to work universally.

I did not invent the different ways one person can be abusive toward another. It is tragic how violent humankind can be. We can trace many countries' histories and the violence that has taken place since the beginning of recorded time.

Gray Areas

When most of us think of domestic abuse, we think of physical assault. Many also think of sexual assault. However, there are other kinds of abuse that are considered gray areas. Some people would not even call them abuse. Others might say this is the way we talk or the way we were raised. Some may argue that if these gray areas are indeed considered abuse that would make us all "abusers." Scary point. These gray areas of abusive behavior are some of the most challenging to address in *The House.*

It's time to build *The House.* Stories and views from both men and women are included to provide real-life examples of what might occur in each room. Let's get started with the first room in *The House.*

ROOM #1. PHYSICAL ABUSE

How does someone abuse someone physically?

Men's View

Notice that I would begin with the question "How does someone abuse someone physically?" I didn't ask, "How have *you* abused someone?" That question will come soon enough. The men were usually able to identify forms of physical abuse. Actions like hit, shove, push, grab, punch, slap, kick, and so on. The words were written in the physical abuse room in *The House*.

There are other forms of physical abuse: actions like tearing clothes, pulling hair, choking, destroying property, stabbing, shooting, or killing.

Men talked about their short fuses or quick tempers as a justification for their actions. Some men would claim these traits were part of their heritage or culture. It's just one more excuse to justify someone's abusive behaviors. These justifications led us to Foundation Statement number one: "I am responsible for my own behavior."

The Short Fuse

In one of my groups, I remember a man in his mid- to late forties. He was soft spoken and appeared very uncomfortable being in the group. He did not contribute to any of the early discussions, but sat quietly and listened to what the other members had to say. Not until after the men built *The House* did he share his story.

"I always had a short fuse. I spanked, I slapped, I grabbed my daughter to discipline her when she was misbehaving. One day when she was not doing what I wanted, I grabbed her and shook her. She went limp. I didn't know what happened, so I took her to the emergency room, where she died. She hemorrhaged and was dead.

"I went to prison. I would give anything if I could just turn back the clock to when I decided to shake her. There isn't a day that goes by that I don't think of her and what I did. It happened over fifteen years ago."

As the men in the group listened to his story, you could have heard a pin drop. The fellow group members did not know what to say. Their heads were lowered, their eyes looking at the floor.

The question for the group was: "Do you think this man planned for this to happen to his daughter?" The group answer was "no."

The Lesson

The lesson here is that when a person decides to resort to putting hands on someone, there is no real way of knowing what might happen. Never did this man think of the tragedy that would result from his physical act of abuse. Now he lives a lifetime of regret. Yes, one could say it was an "accident." But we know the act of physical abuse is a choice, not an accident.

For the vast majority of the men I worked with, physical abuse was a childhood norm. The abuse was typically at the hands of their fathers. Many of these same men said, "At times, I deserved it." "It was discipline, not abuse." Some of them grew up in homes where physical abuse was described as a form of discipline. This approach carried over into their own lives as adults. Ironically, men would say that none of this physical discipline harmed them. Yet they were sitting in a treatment group for abusing their partners and/or their children. People can be seriously injured or die when physical abuse is the choice. These are just the facts.

Women's View

Women who have been physically abused are keenly aware of the dangers of the abuse. They have been hospitalized or suffered miscarriages. Many have fled from their homes in the middle of the night or stood between their abusive partners and their children.

One woman told of being handcuffed naked to the bathroom sink by her partner while he left for the evening. Others reported having guns held to their heads. Weapons in the bedroom and threats of being killed were commonplace for many women.

Women talked about their escape plans. Often the impetus to take action was if they sensed harm to their children. While some of the women would endure the physical abuse to themselves, their children being in harm's way was often the determining factor in deciding to leave the relationship.

Dangerous and Lethal

Physical abuse is a dangerous and potentially lethal act that most people would view as unacceptable. This type of abuse can cause both physical and emotional scars. One comment I heard was "I only hit with an open hand." The fact remains that when physical abuse is used, someone could be injured or die. There were women who if not for a skilled surgeon or an emergency room doctor would be dead.

Physical abuse can provide the evidence needed for the courts to act on behalf of the victims/survivors. As we move to the next rooms in *The House*, we explore other forms of abuse that will not get the attention of law enforcement or the courts. However, these forms of abuse also cause pain and trauma that the victims/survivors may never recover from. These actions cause invisible wounds.

The next three kinds of abuse men commonly named were verbal abuse, mental or psychological abuse, and possibly sexual abuse. If the men struggled with labels, I would help. But I gave them time to identify the abuses on their own. They would come up with other kinds of abuse, like alcohol and drug or child abuse. I asked them to save those categories for later.

ROOM #2. VERBAL ABUSE

How does someone verbally abuse?

Identifying the different kinds of verbal abuse was fairly easy: yelling, screaming, swearing, name calling, put-downs, verbal threats, and so on. This room seems to be pretty easy to fill in, much like the physical abuse room in *The House*. Most people know what verbal abuse sounds like, right?

"You will never amount to anything!" "You are stupid!" "You're worthless!" "You are a terrible father!" "You're an asshole!" These words are from the stories the men told about the verbal abuse they experienced.

I Called Her Names

Usually, as the men start to build *The House*, they begin to express their thoughts about their own situations. Some may blame or accuse their partners, but at times they talk about their own behaviors or memories. One man, who was in Alcoholics Anonymous, shared some of his abusive actions that paired with his issues with alcohol.

"I called her a lot of names, like bitch, slut, whore, fat, stupid, ugly. I know these were bad things to call her. But she would call me names too. When we were both drinking, that's when it got really bad. I know we pressed each other's buttons. Sometimes the verbal attacks got physical. We would argue about stuff and blame each other for who started it."

This is a good example to illustrate the Foundation Statement of the 100 percent rule. If I call her a name, I'm 100 percent responsible. If she calls me a name back, she's 100 percent responsible for her response. If she calls me a name and I don't call her a name back, I won't have a problem. The rule is not 50-50. It's 100-100. I can't assign blame to justify my responsibility.

Men's View

The men could recount stories where others verbally abused them. They had a more difficult time acknowledging their verbal abuse toward their intimate partners. Most men felt their partners were equally or sometimes more capable of verbal abuse. Some admitted that when they felt outmatched verbally, they would resort to physical abuse. The men offered multiple examples of how they used verbal abuse as a nonlethal weapon to harm, degrade, accuse, threaten, blame, and force their partners into doing things to satisfy the man's needs.

Verbal abuse is prevalent in many relationships. It almost seems accepted as just part of our language, as a way we relate when we are upset or frustrated with someone. It's one of those gray areas that some people say is normal in all relationships. We yell at our children when they do something wrong. We argue with our spouses or partners. We say things out of anger or fear, and we regret them later but probably wouldn't consider them to be abusive. Some may argue it's the severity or frequency of the hurtfulness that makes it verbal abuse. We have all heard the saying "Sticks and stones may break my bones, but words will never hurt me." I'll return to this untruth later. Simply stated: words that create hurt are verbal abuse.

Nonverbal Abuse

"Can someone abuse someone nonverbally?" This question is more complicated. The list includes actions like the silent treatment, a look, a stare, or intimidating body language. There are other ways to deploy nonverbal abuse, like using one's physical size difference to intimidate, showing a clenched fist, or pointing a finger.

The men would reluctantly admit verbal and nonverbal abuse occurred. They were often quick to disregard this type of abuse because "she did the same thing." It was viewed as a normal way people talked and argued.

The men used verbal and nonverbal abuse effectively to establish or maintain control and power over their partners. They knew these methods sent a clear message: "If you don't listen to me, I may resort to getting physical." When verbal or nonverbal abuse is used there is little risk of going to jail. But "Two wrongs don't make a right"—another example of the 100 percent rule.

Women's View

In the women's victims/survivors' groups, discussion of verbal and nonverbal abuse yielded a very different response. The women talked about the verbal abuse as being relentless and constant. Some felt it happened almost daily. They said it would happen in front of the children. Others reported it also occurred outside of *The House* in front of friends and family.

The Letter

One task in the women's group is for the women to write a letter to their abuser. Its purpose is to give the women a chance to write down their true feelings about the verbal and nonverbal abuse that has happened to them. The letters are read out loud in the group. One woman exclaimed, "We must all be married to the same man!" What the women choose to do with the letters is up to them. The letters are not intended to be given to their abusive partners. Some kept the letters for future reference. Other women tore up the letter and put it in a wastebasket set in the middle of the group. This powerful exercise is meant to help women rid themselves of the lies their abusers have told them.

The women wrote extensively about all the verbal abuse they endured throughout their relationships with their abusive partners. They identified specific words. The list was endless: stupid, worthless, ugly, fat slob, psycho bitch, cunt, whore, lazy, terrible mother, and more. Women in the group were frequently shocked by the list of what they had been called. The women described how they became accustomed to the verbal abuse and tried to put it out of their minds. But when the words were written down on paper, it became clear how these painful words and accusations cut into their self-worth. Many women talked about how they had been called these things so many times they started to believe them.

A key insight the women learned from this exercise was how much verbal abuse occurred in their relationships. For some women who had never been physically abused and who questioned whether they were in an abusive relationship, this exercise had a major impact. Verbal abuse is an incredibly powerful weapon that often gets forgotten or overlooked by its victims. Women talked about how desensitized they had become to the verbal insults and attacks. For many women, it was as if a light bulb went on when they realized how much verbal abuse they had endured.

The Truth About Words

The next room that will be built, emotional/psychological/mental abuse, will include verbal abuse as well as additional examples of how words can be used to destroy someone. Remember the earlier reference to the adage "Sticks and stones may break my bones, but words can never hurt me"? Well, here's the real truth: "Sticks and stones may break my bones, *but words can last forever."*

Verbal and nonverbal abuse in intimate relationships can usually be traced back to early in the relationship. Women talked about how they now remember incidents of verbal abuse while they were dating their intimate partner. For the women who had not been physically abused, the revelation of how much verbal abuse had occurred was eye-opening.

ROOM #3.
EMOTIONAL/PSYCHOLOGICAL/MENTAL ABUSE

How does someone emotionally/psychologically/mentally abuse?

The third room in *The House* is the emotional/psychological/mental abuse room. These words are used interchangeably in this book. The words and actions described in this room have the greatest potential for devastating, long-lasting effects on victims, and it is the most critical room in *The House*. This room holds an infinite number of stories specific to those who have experienced this kind of abuse.

The Boxer

One group member appeared to become emotional when this third room in *The House* was being discussed. He was in his mid-thirties and had not said much up until this point. The group asked him to talk about what was going on. He spoke about his relationship with his father.

"When I was an adolescent, I got involved in boxing. It became my only interest in life. I loved it, and nothing else mattered. I spent hours in the gym, training to be the best.

"My father was very upset with me. He told me constantly that boxing was a waste of time and that I should be helping him with his work. He always told me I was lazy and wouldn't amount to anything.

"I ended up winning many of my boxing matches and tournaments. I even tried out for the Olympics. My father never came to one of my matches. I never reconciled with my father. He has now passed."

The man thought about this troubled relationship with his father every day. His tears were flowing as he finished his story. The other group members recognized the emotional impact his father's behavior still had on him so many years later. In telling his story, he recognized how his own childhood and adolescent memories applied to his abuse toward his partner and children.

Men's View

The men in the groups sometimes struggled with what fit into this room. This room produces some of the most intense trauma for its victims. The actions it collects are invisible destroyers of the human spirit and psyche. The boxer story helped the men realize what this room entailed. Many of these men had similar experiences from their childhoods and adolescence, and some started to see the connection with their current lives.

Unrecognized Trauma

Fathers, mothers, siblings, teachers, coaches, or significant others sent harmful messages to the men when they were boys and young men. Some of these derogatory, hurtful comments caused serious trauma, most of which had gone unnoticed or unaddressed. The young boxer's father, who called him worthless and never supported his only passion, devastated his son and left a scar the son carried for his whole life.

Men would not describe these statements as causing "trauma." That word was not in their vocabularies. The negative words would be described as "put-downs" or "bad-mouthing." Most men denied giving these comments a second thought. However, they could report what was said to them years or decades earlier as if it happened yesterday. That is the emotional, psychological, and mental power of abusive words.

No Marks Found

This hidden harm makes this room in *The House* critical to explore. There are no physical marks or scars that show someone has been abused. The damage is invisible and goes unnoticed to the public eye. The trauma, often unidentified and untreated, in many instances is irreversible, and its devastation can last a lifetime.

The Worst Kind of Abuse

"What was the worst kind of abuse?" Men gave many different responses to this question. Most exclaimed that physical abuse or child abuse was the worst. Others said it was sexual abuse. Almost without fail, when women were asked this question, they would respond "emotional abuse." It was invisible and its scars last forever. There is little proof of it even happening. The police are not called and the courts do not prosecute. I needed to figure out how to help men recognize emotional abuse in their relationships.

Role Play

Some men recognized the emotional abuse they had experienced. To extend their understanding, I performed a role play to show what emotional abuse they perpetrated against their intimate partners. In this role play, a conversation between a man and his partner, I acted out both parts. It lasted about five minutes. It loses some of its impact in written form, but hopefully the messages are clear.

MAN: "Is that a new dress?"

WOMAN: "Well, I bought it a while back, but this is the first time I've worn it. It was on sale; it was cheap so I bought it."

MAN: "Oh, where did you buy it?"

WOMAN: "I think I bought it at Penney's. Again, it was a while back so I'm not exactly sure."

MAN: "So, where did you get the money to buy it?"

WOMAN: "Well, I had some birthday money my mother gave me, and I had some money from my paycheck. Like I said, it was on sale so it didn't cost much."

MAN: "Does it fit?"

WOMAN: "Yes, I think it fits. Why, what are you saying? Are you saying I'm fat?"

MAN: "No, no, there you go putting words into my mouth again! All I asked was a simple question: does it fit?"

* * *

MAN: "Where are you going?"

WOMAN: "I'm going out for coffee with Kathy."

MAN: "Wait a minute, I got a game tonight! You need to be here with the kids! I don't remember you telling me anything about this. You know I have a game every Wednesday night!"

WOMAN: "Yes, I know you do. That's why I asked you a week ago and you said it wouldn't be a problem if you missed one."

MAN: "No way I said that!"

WOMAN: "Alright, I'm just going to call Kathy and cancel."

MAN: "Kathy. Kathy, is she the woman who has been whoring around with all the guys from her work?"

WOMAN: "What are you talking about? Kathy has been divorced for three years and isn't seeing anybody. Where do you come up with this crap?"

MAN: "Hey, don't blame me. That's just what I've heard."

*   *   *

MAN: "If I'm going to be staying home tonight, I got important things to do. I'm the only one who does anything around here! Did you feed the kids? I ain't got time to be feeding them and getting them to bed!"

WOMAN: "Yes, I fed the kids and got them ready for bed. All you have to do is tuck them in and give a kiss goodnight."

MAN: "Hey, are you taking the car? Because you better put gas in it. If I'm late for work one more time, I'll get canned!"

WOMAN: "I'll put gas in the car."

MAN: "Yeah, well you better get home early, so you and Kathy aren't out all night screwing half the town!"

WOMAN: "No, I'm not going. I've had it. You've already ruined my night. I'm calling Kathy and canceling. You go play your game."

MAN: "No, you'll just be bitching and moaning all night around here. Go on: get the hell out of here! Go and have a good time with your slut friend Kathy!"

After the Role Play

When I finished the role play, there were always interesting verbal and nonverbal responses. Sometimes there were moments of silence or uncomfortable body language and laughter. Other times there were negative comments. Still, even with my bad acting, the message was clear. The men would not admit it, but this example rang true.

ROLE-PLAY QUIZ

I would ask the group, "What was the first question?" Most of the time they didn't remember. I gave them a moment to recall. The first question was "Is that a new dress?"

I then asked, "Is it an abusive question?" The men weren't sure how to answer. I explained that, in and of itself, it's not an abusive question. But what was its underlying meaning or motive? Most of the men knew what was behind this question: past histories of negative comments about her weight or degrading her appearance.

I would add it could be a simple question of interest. But in an abusive relationship, where there is a history of underlying messages, it was not a question of interest. The woman already knew this was not going to go well.

THE DRESS

I continued to ask the group questions about the exchange between the couple. The next line of questioning was about where she bought the dress. And where did she get the money? These two questions pointed to several things. The subject of money frequently is an issue in abusive relationships. Women reported much abuse happened during or after arguments about her spending money.

The woman's answer made clear she needed to justify and account for her actions. Her comment about using some of her money from her paycheck would come into focus later in the role play.

The next question, "Does it fit?" once again could be a question of genuine interest. For example, another response along these lines would be, "Wow, you look great!" But the men knew this was not the message behind this question. The history of degrading the woman's physical appearance or her weight was the real message. The man's quick response, "There you go putting words into my mouth again! All I asked was a simple question," was an all-too-familiar tactic. Many women referred to this approach as "crazy making." They would second-guess themselves, questioning if he really was just asking an innocent question.

THE FRIEND

The next target of attack was the friend and her alleged sexual behaviors. The old saying "Birds of a feather flock together" basically implies that who you hang out with is who you are. Calling Kathy a whore was telling his partner she was one too.

WHOSE JOB IS IT?

The final barrage of questions covered everything from who was responsible for the children to claiming he was the only one who worked. She had already mentioned her own job. Connecting her actions to his potential job loss set the stage so that when he does lose his job, it would be her fault. The gas tank could be overflowing and she would still be blamed. Finally, he refused to let her stay home, telling her to get out and go with her slut friend.

WHAT'S THE BEST TIME?

Then I would ask, "What would be a good time for her to come home tonight?" The men knew exactly what I was asking. This question always produced an interesting exchange of answers. Most of the time the men would agree: "no time" was going to be the "right" time for her to come home.

WHAT WILL HAPPEN?

The final wrap-up for this role play ended with a few last questions. "What do you think will happen when she does get home tonight?" "Would there be the potential for physical, verbal, emotional, or sexual abuse?" "What do you think would happen if he asked her to have sex and she said 'no'?" "Did he ever lay a hand on her during the role-play exchange?" "Did he have to?" "Did he abuse her?"

This five-minute role play worked every time. It generated a very real discussion about how much damage could be caused without any physical abuse involved. It has been one of the most significant interventions to help men see what emotional abuse looks like in a relationship. In less than five minutes they could devastate a person without laying a finger on them.

A Word of Caution

Before I did this role play with the women and with general audiences, I warned it might generate some strong emotions. I made it clear that it was important to take care of themselves. If the emotions became overwhelming, they may choose to leave the room.

When I acted out this role play with general audiences, almost without fail women would come up to me afterward and tell me this role play described their past or present relationship. Men would come up and tell me they believed their mother, sister, or daughter was in an abusive relationship and ask what they should do.

Women Know

When I presented this role play in women's groups, they knew exactly what was behind the first question and what was coming next.

The women said it was a powerful example they could relate to in telling their experiences of emotional abuse. Women who had not been physically abused would question if they were really a "battered woman." Many initially wondered if they belonged in the group. This role play helped them recognize the abuse they had endured.

HER THINGS

There are many ways that emotional/psychological/mental abuse is used in intimate partner relationships. Threats and actions to destroy her favorite things or kill her cat are some of the ways men try to control and have power over their partners.

HER CONTRIBUTIONS

Often the woman would be blamed for the family's financial struggles. She would be accused of not "carrying her load" because she was at home and not working, although all of the household duties, including caring for the children, were hers. In addition, when she did try to go outside of the home to work or school, he would often sabotage her efforts.

HER BODY

Often the examples of emotional/psychological/mental abuse included degrading a partner's body or sexual performance. Accusing her of having affairs or comparing her to past lovers is a common tactic. Attacking her body image and physical appearance is a powerful way to destroy a partner's self-confidence. All this was done without raising a hand.

MOTHERHOOD

The women talked about their partners telling them they were "a bad mother." The men would often blame them for all the troubles with the children. Attacking her as an inadequate mother was a significant demoralizing experience, the women reported, and self-doubt about their motherhood became an issue.

Emotional/psychological/mental abuse toward partners can be subtle or not so subtle. It can be sophisticated or unsophisticated. This type of abuse is always aimed directly at the jugular vein. The abuser knows the most vulnerable points for their partners and attacks there. These actions can be described as "mind games" or "head games."

Am I Really a Victim?

As described earlier in the verbal abuse room in *The House*, women who had not been physically abused questioned if they were really a "battered woman." They would ask if this women's group was the right place for them. Many women who have been seriously emotionally abused do not seek help as a "battered woman."

ROOM #4. SEXUAL ABUSE

How does somebody sexually abuse?

I can't recall an actual story that any of the men told about their sexual abuse toward their intimate partner. In contrast, the women frequently described a history of the sexual abuse that had occurred in their relationships.

Out for Cigarettes

One woman told this story in the group. She was in her late twenties and had been in a long-term relationship. A friend had told her about the women's group. She wasn't sure it was the right kind of group for her, but she decided to check it out. When the group was filling in the sexual abuse room in *The House*, she said her boyfriend would send her out to buy his cigarettes. He would expect her back in ten minutes. If she returned even a minute late, he would accuse her of "screwing half the city."

Men's View

This room was always a challenge. A few men would talk about how the sex was the only good thing about their relationship. Others said there had always been problems in the sexual relationship with their partner. Men talked about "sweet-talking her" into having sex. They also complained about no sex or her withholding sex. Men would say it's man's nature to have sex. If he wasn't getting his sexual needs met with his partner, he would be justified in getting his needs met elsewhere.

A common theme in the men's groups was the men were suspicious and accused their partner of having affairs. They also claimed their partners would accuse them of the same.

One night the men asked one of the group members who had constantly talked about his partner having an affair if he had any proof. The man said, "no." The group pressed him: did he really believe she was having an affair? He finally said that he didn't think so. The group continued with the question "Are you having an affair?" After much denial, he reluctantly answered, "yes." He said that by accusing her of having an affair, he felt he was keeping her on the defensive and he would not get caught.

Women's View

Women would often describe their sexual relationships in different terms. Many of the women said that sex was a major problem in the relationship. Most talked about experiencing on a regular basis degrading comments and pressure to have sex. Common examples included being told "it's your duty" or being asked "if you aren't having sex with me, who are you having sex with?" Negative messages about her body or sexual performance and comparisons to past partners were constantly used against her. The women also reported their partner's relentless accusations of her having an affair. Women often spoke about struggles when their partner wanted to have sex after he had abused her verbally or even physically. Often, they would have sex just to end the argument or so they were able to go to sleep.

A Story Men Know

To illustrate for the men an example of sexual abuse, I made up a story that might help them think about what sexual messages and attitudes boys and young men are taught in our society.

I would start by asking, "How many of you have a teen-age son? For those of you who don't, pretend you have a thirteen-year-old son. You just found out that the forty-year-old neighbor woman has been having sex with your thirteen-year-old son. What would you do?"

You can probably guess their response. I told the men to be honest. After some uncomfortable laughter, the men would come up with their answers: "Right on, son!" "Go for it!" "I wish it would have happened to me!"

Then I asked, "How many of you have a thirteen-year-old daughter?" Yes, you know what's coming. "I want you to pretend you have a thirteen-year-old daughter. You just found out that the forty-year-old neighbor man has been having sex with your thirteen-year-old daughter. What would you do?"

"Kill him!" "Cut off his dick and balls . . . slowly!"

I would then ask, "If this was a women's group, what do you think they would say about these two situations?" Most of the men responded that the women would be very upset in both cases.

I have told this story in women's groups. Their reactions are exactly what the men knew they would be. The women were appalled, disgusted, outraged, and saddened by the men's responses.

How Did This Happen?

I would ask the men, "How do you think we got here as men?" They were hard-pressed to come up with answers. I let them know not all men think this way. But far too many do. The majority of the men in the groups knew these two scenarios would be equally wrong and harmful to both their sons and daughters. "Are men born this way?" "Did our fathers or mothers teach us this attitude?" "Did we learn it from the movies, video games, or television?" "Did we learn it from other men?" "How long has it been like this?" "What have been the consequences or benefits of these sexual attitudes and beliefs?" "Will you pass down these same beliefs to your sons and daughters?" In the end, the men agreed both scenarios were acts of sexual abuse.

Sexual Abuse Is More Than Rape

Rape, forced or unwanted sex, and inappropriate touching are all forms of sexual abuse. But there are more ways to abuse someone sexually. Affairs are one of the most frequent issues discussed in the groups. False accusations and actual affairs are common in abusive relationships.

Other ways to sexually abuse someone include actions that were identified in the verbal and emotional/psychological/mental rooms in *The House*. The walls in *The House* are very thin, and the rooms oftentimes overlap. Degrading a partner's body, making derogatory comments about anything sexual in the relationship, verbally abusing, mentally abusing, and physically abusing can all be present in the sexual abuse room. The list goes on: pornography; how women are portrayed in movies, on television, or in video games; comparison to past lovers; and being made to perform unwanted sexual acts are all forms of sexual abuse.

Marital Rape

I would address one more aspect of sexual abuse in intimate relationships. By 1993, all fifty states and DC had enacted laws against marital rape. When I was facilitating domestic abuse groups in the early '80s, few states had marital rape laws. Until 1976, it was reported every state had a "marital exemption" that allowed a husband to rape his wife without fear of legal consequences. Still today, states treat spousal rape differently depending upon the case. Even with laws in place, marital rape is still difficult to prosecute and convict. Yet, nonconsensual sexual intercourse between non-spouses has always been illegal (National Coalition Against Domestic Violence).

Women's Doubts

Many women who have experienced different kinds of sexual abuse do not think this abuse makes them a victim of domestic violence. Once again, unfortunately, the term "battered woman" is frequently thought of as only physical abuse.

Making a List

An exercise originally used in the women's group was later added in the men's groups. The group members make a list of negative names that men called women and women called men. The words and names were very revealing.

The list of things men called women was overwhelmingly focused on negative sexual descriptions, as women enumerated on page 43 in the "letter" exercise. The list of what women called men was far less sexual and less negative. It was also shorter. This contrast was a stark example of how much sexual abuse is present in abusive relationships that do not involve rape or unwanted physical touch.

Rare Disclosure

Rarely, men would bring up being sexually abused in their childhood or adolescence. If someone did acknowledge such abuse, group members had a very difficult time knowing how to respond. I informed the group that boys and young men were sexually abused as well and how few sought help. I encouraged them to seek help if they had been victims. I offered to meet with them at any time in private and offered other resources for future counseling if they chose to seek additional help.

I reminded the fathers in the group that their sons and daughters were at risk of being sexually abused. I encouraged them to talk with their children about this issue. It is a subject still avoided in many households. The secret remains, and the trauma never is addressed.

The Difference

Filling in the sexual abuse room in *The House* could take many turns. There were major differences between what the men talked about versus the women. The men blamed their partners for the sexual problems in their relationships and projected onto them. The women took a deeper look at the impact of all the ways they had been sexually abused.

ROOM #5. INTIMIDATION

How does a person use intimidation to abuse?

Only to Scare

One young man did not resemble many of the other men in the group. He was slight in build and appeared to be somewhat intimidated by the other members. He did not express any anger about being in the group and sat quietly, as if he wanted to go unnoticed. After several sessions, he told his story of why he was ordered to attend the group.

"I recently got married. I have been told I have a temper. It was more like a volcano. I would let things build up, and then I would explode. I never would get physical with my wife, but I would throw things around the house to intimidate her.

"I destroyed her things and did things to scare her. Sometimes while eating dinner, we would get into an argument and I would throw a plate of food on the floor or against the wall.

"One night at the kitchen table, I grabbed a pop can and threw it toward her, aiming at the kitchen wall behind her. My hand slipped. The can hit her in the face. The tab on the can caught her in the eye. I took her to the emergency room, where they tried to save my wife's eye. But they couldn't save it. She now has a glass eye. Every day when I look at her, I'm reminded of what I did. It's something I will have to live with the rest of my life." Like the man who unintentionally killed his young daughter, this man too wished he could turn back the clock.

The group members hesitantly started asking him some questions. "Are you still married?" "What does she tell people when they ask what happened?" "What do her parents think?" "Did you get arrested?" It was a very sad yet powerful example of how quickly things can go terribly wrong. He said he only meant to scare her to get what he wanted.

Women's View

Women shared some of the intimidating comments their partners have made: "I'm going to kill you!" "I'm going to kill myself!" "I will kill you, me, and the kids!" "You leave me, I will take the children and you will never see them again!" "I will kill the dog!" "I will divorce you and you will have nothing!" "Good luck finding someone with your fat ass and four kids!"

One woman described an incident when her husband was in the bedroom with a gun threatening to kill himself. She was panic-stricken and called the police. He went into the garage and poured gasoline over himself. He came back into the house and threatened to set himself on fire. Meanwhile, their two young children were in the bedroom, unaware of what was happening. She feared he would light himself on fire and the children would watch their father burn to death. She also feared he would set the house on fire and all of them would perish.

By the time the police arrived, her husband had showered and acted as if nothing had happened. He started schmooz-ing and joking with the officers, denying that anything was wrong. She, on the other hand, was frantically trying to explain to the police what had transpired. She said, "I could still smell the gasoline; couldn't they smell it?" It was another example of the "crazy making" experience when the abuser looks normal and the woman is viewed as irrational. The police told him to take a walk around the block, and they left. A half hour later she was face-to-face with her hus-band as he screamed at her and made more threats.

Threats of suicide and homicide are common in abusive relationships. Other forms of intimidation such as threats of divorce or taking the children also extract a heavy toll on women trying to navigate these situations.

Men's View

Men will sometimes admit to making one of these threats toward their partner. This confession often is followed with "I was just joking." "I was drunk." "I never said that!"

The bottom line is women and children don't think of it as joking. They have seen the anger and violent acts in the past and are afraid the threats could become reality. Other acts of intimidation include menacing looks, threatening body posture, and verbal and nonverbal threats. Men sometimes may not even be aware of how they appear to their partners or children, but the women and children know that "look."

Stalking

Research shows one in six women has been stalked by an intimate partner during her lifetime (National Coalition Against Domestic Violence, 2017; National Intimate Partner and Sexual Violence Survey, 2010 summary report). This type of intimidation is another kind of abuse causing psychological trauma and fear in the victims' daily lives.

All Inclusive

The intimidation room could be included in several other rooms in *The House*. It uses many of the same words and actions as the emotional/psychological/mental room. It can combine physical, verbal, emotional, and sexual abuse all into one.

ROOM #6. MALE PRIVILEGE

What is male privilege?

Men struggled with what to place in this room. When they were challenged with the evidence that all men, including myself, have male privilege, a great deal of discussion transpired. It was very important to spend time talking about how this privilege had impacted their relationships with their partners.

The Hunting Story

I created a role play to help the men recognize male privilege.

MAN: "Hey honey, it's November and it's time to go deer hunting with my dad, my brother, and uncles. It's our annual hunt. I just bought a new gun and new gear. We got plenty of whiskey and beer. You have the kids. Give them a kiss for me. I'll be back in three days. See you later!"

Now for the flip side. It goes something like this:

WOMAN: "Hey honey, it's July and my sister, some women friends, and I are renting a cabin at a resort on the lake. I bought a new swimming suit and a few more things for our trip. We've got plenty of wine and beer. You have the kids. Give them a hug and kiss for me. I'll be back in three days!"

There was much uncomfortable laughter and mumbling from the men. They might claim ignorance, but they knew exactly what this room was about. They didn't even need to be a hunter to get the message. When I presented this scenario in the women's groups, the participants understood it within the first sentence.

The King

The most common examples of male privilege are sayings like the man is the boss, the head of the house, the bread-winner, or the king of the castle. Other characteristics men claimed to be true include "Men are smarter than women, are stronger than women, do more work than women, and are more important."

More Privilege

Here are other simple examples of male privilege: When men go into a dark parking lot to their cars, are they worried they may get raped? As they walk down the street, do men get sexual comments or wolf whistles from women that make them uncomfortable? How about the double standard that exists for men versus women? If a man has several women, he is a "stud." If a woman has several men, she's a "whore" or "slut." There is the double standard of male privilege that says men can stay out late and hang out at the bar or clubs. After all, that's what men do. What about women? Does the same freedom apply?

Often the men would say things like, "She can go out any-time she wants." "I let her go out clubbing with her friends all the time." What men don't say is what happens when she gets home.

The Jacket

One night in the women's group a woman told her story about wanting to buy a leather jacket. A professional with a good-paying job, she had the funds to purchase the jacket without any problem.

She decided she would train to run a marathon and treat herself with the jacket if she achieved her goal. She ran the race and bought the jacket. Remember the role play when the woman bought the dress? This woman told her story after hearing the role play. She knew when she bought the jacket what she would encounter if she ever wore it. The jacket remained hidden in a closet where her partner wouldn't see it. The history of having to justify and explain her purchases to her partner was not worth it. She decided not to put herself through it and never wore her jacket.

Women's View

The women talked about struggles with their partner's frequent interrogations and false accusations. They knew they would have to answer "twenty questions" accounting for their whereabouts and spending. It's possible every type of abuse in *The House* might occur before the night ended.

The women told frequent stories of situations where they had to explain or justify their purchases. In stark contrast, their male partners could spend and do as they pleased. It was the male's privilege to do so.

In healthy relationships, roles get assigned or assumed, intentionally or unintentionally. Here are several examples of questions I asked of the men: "Who is the primary caretaker for the children?" "Who does the major cooking and cleaning?" "Who is responsible for grocery shopping?" "Who controls the money?" "Who fixes the car?" "Who does the house maintenance?" "Who makes the major buying decisions?" "Who decides who does these jobs?"

Men's View

When the men talked about their views on money management and gender roles it was usually from a vantage of male privilege. They would defend their actions by saying things like, "I make more money and I will decide how to spend it." Or they would claim that her judgment about spending is poor or out of control and needs to be monitored. Again, the men would claim their tasks as more important or valuable and minimize and devalue her assigned duties.

Historically, some traditional gender roles have been assigned to women or men. Many have fallen by the wayside, but some are still in place today. The question is not "Who should be assigned these roles or duties?" but rather "How are they assigned?" Who made the major money decisions or controlled the spending was one role that could involve male privilege. In healthy relationships, ideally the roles would be talked about and agreed upon by both parties. In abusive relationships, the man commonly determined the roles. Often these assigned duties were acts of power and control over the woman. Some roles were meant to keep women in their place or give her the duties he didn't want. He most likely defined these jobs as "women's work." The division of labor between the couple clearly showed examples of gender roles and male privilege.

ROOM #7. SOCIAL ISOLATION

How does someone use social isolation to abuse?

Women's Work

One member said he did not see anything that looked like abuse in his childhood home. He had grown up in a white, working-class neighborhood in the '50s. His accounting for what took place seemed normal.

"I remember growing up my father wouldn't let my mother go out of the house. He said he was the breadwinner and her job was to stay home and take care of the house and kids. He didn't want her talking to her mother or sisters or visiting any of her friends. He felt her time needed to be spent doing the cooking and cleaning and watching the children. It seemed like my mother accepted her role and never really complained about it. To me, everything seemed normal.

"Later on, when all of us kids were grown, they got a divorce. I asked her why. She told me she was never happy and felt very alone. There were times, she said, when she would secretly see her mother and her friends, just to have some contact with the outside world. I never really thought much about her needs. It just seemed like the house and taking care of kids is what a woman does."

There are many homes where women are the primary caretakers of the household and do the kinds of things this man thought were normal. There are homes where these roles are carried out and there is no abuse. Perhaps this woman may even have family or friends with whom she has some social connection. But in the scenario this man described as "normal," it's obvious that not all things were happy.

Carrying Her Weight

Members of the women's groups talked about trying to hold a job or go to school. A woman related that one of the main arguments she had in her relationship was about money. Her partner constantly told her that she needed to "carry her weight" and go get a job. The fact that she was the primary caretaker for their five children and the house was not important.

Hoping to end the argument, she decided to get a job. The story went on. He was now yelling that the house was a mess, she was an unfit mother for neglecting the children, and dinner was never on time. In addition, he would stalk her at work. He called her at work several times a day, telling her she was a "worthless bitch." In reality, he didn't want her working or socializing outside of the home.

Keeping the Secret

Social isolation is a critical strategy to maintain control over a person's whereabouts and their contacts. It keeps the "secret" of the abuse inside the four walls. If the abused partner gets out of the house, she might start telling her story to someone. She may end up getting support to leave or get a court order for protection. She may get a job and become independent. It seemed the men's number-one fear was she might find someone who treated her better. I would say to them, "Whether you want to believe it or not, it's true. The harsh reality is it won't take much to find your replacement."

Not letting a partner go to work or school are common ways that men keep their power. Restricting her from seeing friends or family, not letting her have a phone or access to the car, and controlling the money keep her isolated from her support. The list goes on. All of these actions are ways men keep the "secret" and control their partner's activities. Women have reported some unbelievable but true stories about how their partners have isolated them from the outside world—everything from removing the car's spark plugs to handcuffing them to the bathroom sink.

Rural Isolation

The women in the group who lived in rural communities reported unique issues of social isolation. They were even more at risk of not having access to resources to help them escape an abusive situation. In rural areas people knew each other's business. If a woman were to seek help from law enforcement or the church, she could be exposed to the whole community, making the situation more dangerous for her. She might remain silent so as not to risk exposure. In addition, she might be worried about damaging her partner's reputation in the community.

Most small towns don't have the counseling resources available for a woman to seek help. She may have to drive several hours to find shelter or support. If she did not have access to a vehicle or funds to get away, she likely would remain trapped in her home with little hope for a way out. If she were able to seek counseling, she would have to account for where she had gone. In a small community, all of these issues needed to be considered for the woman's safety.

The Suburbs

In the suburbs, the walls are thicker. The houses are farther apart than in the city. The neighbors don't hear the yelling and screaming. Nobody ever thinks that domestic abuse happens in the suburbs. Women from these middle-class neighborhoods talked about hiding their bruises. They were ashamed of what was happening in their "picture-perfect homes." Rarely had police been called to their homes to respond to a reported domestic incident. It was unusual to have any court involvement.

Some talked about having access to more resources, like private therapists and marriage counselors. However, many women reported their therapists did not adequately address the abuse.

One alarming concern is the number of men who are never identified as abusers and continue to abuse their intimate partners. Their children witness and experience the same traumas as those who are less privileged as a result of their economic or cultural status. Typically, these men are white, middle- or upper-middle-class males who will never suffer any consequences for their abusive behaviors. They are business executives, politicians, skilled trade workers, and other professionals who are well hidden from the criminal justice system. We served only a very few of these men in our program. However, there were several of their victims/ survivors in the women's groups. The women told stories of their partners who remained hidden in the sanctity of their suburban homes. Many of these men will continue to go undetected and rarely acknowledge or seek help for their abuse. The news media has exposed some high-profile individuals, yet many still go untouched by the law. Unfortunately, the women in these types of relationships most likely will need to take action on their own to protect themselves and their children from their perpetrators.

Urban Neighborhoods

The opposite can be true in urban communities. The living spaces are closer together, and frequently the neighbors have developed strong interpersonal relationships. Their children play and go to school together, and there is a greater chance that people will know each other's business. These factors may make it more difficult for neighbors to involve themselves in the issues families are experiencing in the privacy of their own homes. Reporting a domestic incident could result in a major conflict for those involved.

Minority Communities' Response

In communities of color, other barriers are in play. There can be a reluctance to call the police for fear of their response. There are many reasons domestic abuse is not reported in minority communities. The systems that are meant to protect victims often do not work for communities of color. Additional factors must be considered before a woman of color chooses to report her abuser. Historical experiences of what happens when police respond in communities of color have been and continue to be a deterrent to having the police intervene. Women of color know if the police respond to their call, their abuser will likely be treated more harshly in the courts than his white counterparts.

The Police Response

I had many opportunities to work with civilian and military police to discuss the police response to domestic calls. The majority of the officers reported that these were some of the most difficult and volatile situations they would encounter. During the thirty years I worked with law enforcement, many practices and policies regarding police response to domestic assaults changed. In the end, there were vast improvements to educate and support police to better respond to these extremely complex situations.

Control by Isolation

Social isolation is a powerful instrument to keep women from seeking support and to keep the secret of abuse hidden from view. Women's stories of what their partners did to control their movements are endless. Often they reported how they had to find creative ways to maintain any outside interactions.

The common themes of controlling the money, the car, her job, and her social contacts were all ways he was able to control her life. Women talked about being caretakers, making sure everyone's needs were met—except their own. The thought of leaving the relationship had crossed women's minds numerous times, yet they felt a deep sense of responsibility to stay and keep things from falling apart. The women in the groups had relationships and marriages ranging from six months to thirty years. Those in the long-term relationships revealed their regrets of not acting sooner. They encouraged others to seriously consider their options and not live a life in fear and despair.

ROOM #8. RELIGION

How does someone use religion to abuse?

Religion can be a powerful force in people's lives. It can be the basis for staying in a relationship or ending one. In my experience, religion, faith, and spirituality was talked about more in the women's groups than in the men's. In men's groups, religion or spirituality was not a main topic of concern. Some men did reference Scriptures or cultural and religious beliefs as a reason or justification for the abuse. Although historically an argument could be made that some religious teachings were abusive, no religious teaching, be it the Bible, an organized religion, or a religious or spiritual figure, should be used to condone violence against another human being. One would hope this tenet holds true for all cultures.

The Bible Says

I have heard men exclaim, "It says in the Bible women are supposed to be servants to the man!" "He is the master!" "The Scriptures say women are inferior to men and they are put on this earth to satisfy the man." "Our religion states in the marriage vows the woman is to honor and obey her husband, till death do us part." "If you divorce me, you will go to hell!" "You are not a Christian." "Have you ever heard about spare the rod, spoil the child?" "Spanking my child is what the Scriptures tell me to do!"

Men's View

These statements have been made by men who choose to use religion or faith as a justification for their abuse. The use of religion as a way to abuse someone should not be all that surprising. Religious differences throughout history have been at the center of much violence and death.

In most of the men's groups I have facilitated, the majority of the men didn't practice or have much interest in a faith or religious affiliation. If religion was one of their partner's vulnerable areas, they used it as another tactic to control her. Men also used misinterpretations of the Bible enumerated in the above paragraph. One question I posed was "Who wrote the Bible?" "Men?" Also, "Do any of these teachings condone abuse of women or children?"

Women's View

Women talked more about their faith and spirituality than the men. For some women religion was a very significant part of their lives. These women would talk about believing their faith told them to stay in the relationship and to honor their marriage vows. Women believed that prayer and devotion and trust in their faith would help them through their troubled times.

Seeking Help from the Church

A person's religion or spiritual beliefs may be a key factor in why someone might stay in an abusive relationship. In these cases, it is important to address this issue. However, it is also critical *how* it might be addressed.

Many faith institutions have failed to adequately recognize or confront abuse in intimate relationships. Women reported that when they went to their minister, priest, or rabbi for marriage counseling, abuse was never addressed. No questions about abuse were asked. If the subject did surface, it was not the primary focus. The abuse remained a secret. The counseling often took the approach that more prayer or church involvement would be the best solution for resolving the couple's marital issues. Women reported they were told to go home and be a "better wife" and realize the pressures their husband had at his job to support his family. Or, if she did report the abuse, the minister's response might be, "Not Robert! He is a pillar in this church!" Women who attended the women's groups talked about the stark difference in this counseling experience compared to what they received through their church.

When someone in an abusive relationship seeks help, it is important to know who will provide the help. In many counseling settings, it is still a goal to keep couples together. This approach is especially true for some religious institutions.

I made it clear in counseling both the men and the women that my role was not to pull people apart, and neither was it to keep them together. My goal was to help the man or woman examine their relationship and decide for themselves what they wanted to do.

In recent years there has been more training for clergy on what questions to ask to help uncover abuse in relationships. Fortunately, more clergy have become informed of the prevalence of intimate partner abuse.

ROOM #9. CHILD ABUSE

Do you think children can be abused in all of these ways?

The answer was always a very quick "yes" from all of the men in the group.

A Childhood Memory

One of the more revealing stories was told by a man who vividly recalled his greatest fear of childhood. It was as if he had an epiphany regarding what really took place during his life as a young boy.

"I remember growing up with my brother and my mother, who raised us after our father left. My mother was very strict. She believed we needed to be raised with firm discipline, given we didn't have a father figure.

"She used to spank us using different objects, like a wooden spoon or a switch or a piece of Hot Wheels race car track. I remember that this happened often since my brother and I would do things to get in trouble.

"She was very overweight, and when my brother and I got older, we could run away from her and avoid the physical beating. However, that didn't stop the spankings. At night when my brother and I went to sleep, she would come in and hit us in our beds. I remember there were many nights when I would try to stay awake, not knowing if I had done something wrong that day and she might come in to beat me.

"I always thought it was her just being strict. My brother and I thought we deserved it. I figured that's what happens when we disobey or do something wrong.

"Now I know what my wife and kids are feeling. They never know what I'm going to do or when. They are experiencing the same thing I did as a kid. I never knew what was going to happen. I remember that I was afraid a lot of nights. I really haven't thought about it much, but now I realize it was probably child abuse. I still have occasional nightmares about those nights."

A Different Lens

By now, hopefully some men were looking at their own abuse through a different lens. It was encouraging to see them reflecting on the kinds of abuse they witnessed and endured in their childhood homes. Some began to share their childhood experiences. Others would nod their heads or remain silent.

Reflecting on their abusive childhoods helped the men begin to feel some empathy and compassion for their victims. Unfortunately, many were still not willing to see past their anger toward their partners. But there was still time for them to examine their abusive behaviors. It was only the end of the second session.

One man said he had been in two previous relationships, both ending due to his abuse. He had always blamed the woman for the breakup. On the third relationship, now ending, he realized he was the only common denominator. He admitted he was abusive in his past relationships. His primary reason for ending his abusive behavior was he didn't want his young son to be a victim of his abuse.

Men's View

Child abuse is the unthinkable kind of abuse. The quick "yes" in all men's groups tells us they know children can be abused in all these ways. Given most of the men's childhood histories, it seems they should be more than eager to end abuse in their own *House*. Unfortunately, this is often not the case. Most continue to defend, deny, and justify many of their abusive behaviors. However, a few are ready to take a first step in a lifetime commitment to make a real change.

What Does It Feel Like?

"What do you think it feels like, being a child living in this *House*?" The men would say things like, "It's scary, it's bad, and it sucks." They might even say the children living in this *House* are afraid and feel helpless. At this point, some of the men may have begun to think back on their own childhood memories or feelings of what it was like to live in a *House* like this one.

What Do the Children Want?

"What do you think the children want?" Children love both of their parents, and they don't want to see them hurt each other. They are afraid something bad will happen. It's probably not the first time they have witnessed this scene. They know bad things have happened. Often children in abusive homes think the abuse is their fault. Parents may even have told them it's their fault. Feelings of guilt or helplessness are common for children living in *The House*. All the children want is for it to stop. If I really wanted to find out the truth about what was happening in *The House*, I would ask the children.

The Buck Stops Here

It is sad and tragic that children have to live in a *House* like this one. It is hard not to have empathy and compassion for those who grew up under these circumstances. This violent upbringing is the reality for many, if not most, of the men in treatment for domestic violence. There is nothing to be done to change the past experiences for these men. The goal of treatment is to help them examine their pasts in an effort to help them change things in the present and future. They can apply the message "the buck stops here." It's up to the individual to end the abuse for the sake of the children, the partner, and themselves. This firsthand experience of living in *The House* should motivate the person to change that scenario. Sadly, in most cases that is not what happens.

Such men need to face the Fourth Foundation Statement: "The only person I can control is myself." It is up to them to decide what the rest of their lives will look like. The choice to recognize and end their abuse is solely in their control. If they continue to try to control others with their abusive behaviors in whatever form, their lives and those around them will continue to be damaged.

Stuck in the Middle

In relationships involving children, the men likely would continue to have some kind of connection to them. What would the man's role be? Would he blame the children's mother for all the problems and take no responsibility for his behavior?

The familiar phrase "putting kids in the middle" described many of these failed relationships. This situation was a major concern for mothers. Women often reported the terrible scenarios involving the children that occurred after an abusive relationship ended.

The children struggled with understanding their parents' volatile relationship and were afraid of what might happen next. Children often felt at fault for the problems between their parents. Some were told they were the reason for the problems. The children's fears and anxieties led to other serious school, mental, and physical health issues.

Children living in abusive homes were undiscovered victims. The women talked about their fears of what impact the abuse would have on their children. They were worried about their sons turning into abusers like their fathers. They were also concerned about not having a father figure in the home.

The men were frustrated and angry. Some were sad and worried about the children. They all claimed they loved their children and wouldn't do anything to harm them. Yet they failed to recognize their own abusive behavior and the trauma it caused. They continued to cast blame on their partners for the breakup of the family.

Visitation, custody battles, and child support issues were major points of concern. Men reported they were not allowed to see their children and were angered by their limited rights as a father. At the same time, many of them had violated the conditions set by the courts. Many expressed open hostilities directed at the mothers and felt they had little say in their children's lives.

On these hot-button issues, the group leader might solicit the members' help to calm a man's anger and think of peaceful solutions. Some men were able to offer appropriate and thoughtful options. They would encourage nonviolent and responsible legal actions.

Some men fed into this anger and joined the attack on women and the system. It is critical that the counselors defuse this perspective and confront the negative comments, at the same time encouraging the men who offer positive suggestions and support. The strength of a group treatment approach is to use the power of the group members' positive voices. Their words can have the most credibility and influence over fellow participants. It is always a challenge to stop the negative voices, which frequently are the loudest, especially in the early phases of the group process. However, when positive voices surface, they have an amazing effect. This is why counseling groups are our program's primary service model for perpetrators and victims/survivors. In group treatment, it is crucial to use the positive power of group members' voices. They are the ones who will be listened to.

CHAPTER SIX

After *The House*

This chapter provides a summary of what happens after *The House* has been built. It poses some important final questions for the men. It also describes some additional "rooms" that could be added to *The House*.

Finished

The group members had built *The House*. The men had completed session two of the sixteen-week journey. In most instances, the tone of the group had changed from its volatile beginning. Some men had shared their personal experiences and had admitted to acts of abuse. Voices were lowered and less-defensive postures were visible. Usually a number of men appeared to be in a better place.

The main purpose of *The House* is to help the men see the various ways they abuse their intimate partners. The exercises and stories help the men begin to see things from a different perspective. I might ask of the group: "What did you learn from this exercise?" The men's comments would be telling. The responses ranged from "this is what she does to me" to "I never really thought about all these things as abuse." Building *The House* also provides a look back at their childhoods. Most of them had never confronted the abuse they had survived.

Building *The House* provided them with a nonthreatening way to examine their personal past and present situations. The power of a group is why group treatment versus individual counseling is so important for men who abuse their intimate partners. The role of the group facilitator is to guide and utilize the participants' positive contributions. The negative contributions must be discouraged and stopped. This guidance takes skill and leadership. Group facilitators must remember that the words of a group member have more meaning than anything a counselor could ever say. It is critical that the facilitator knows how to use the positive power of the group.

The rooms of *The House* are now filled in, but there are still some important questions to ask.

Worst Kind of Abuse

When the rooms were complete, the next question posed to the men was: "What is the worst kind of abuse?" When I asked this question earlier, their answers varied: child abuse, sexual abuse, or physical abuse were frequent responses.

It's a trick question. The reality is they are all bad. All of these kinds of abuse destroy relationships. People get traumatized, are hurt, or die. This abuse is not against strangers or enemies. It's against the people the men love or loved.

Second question: "What do you think women say is the worst kind of abuse?" Again, the men would make their guesses. I would tell them the women's number-one answer is emotional abuse. All abuse hurts. Emotional abuse cuts the deepest and lasts the longest. Physical abuse leaves marks or scars. It can also cause injury and death. With emotional abuse, there are no visible marks. The wounds are all on the inside. The victims/survivors live with those memories for the rest of their lives.

Women describe emotional abuse as being "crazy making." There is no proof or physical evidence any abuse has occurred. The mind games wear a person down. The abuse is totally directed at the woman's most vulnerable areas: false accusations of having affairs; constant attacks on her body image; derogatory name calling; telling her she is a bad mother or she is stupid and worthless.

House for Sale

Next question: "If a real estate agent wanted to sell you this *House*, would you buy it?" "How about if all of the rooms were cleaned except for one?" Most of the men agreed they wouldn't want to buy it.

Here's the hardest part of ending domestic violence. If someone cleans out the physical abuse room and the sexual abuse room and so on, but doesn't clean out *all* of the rooms in *The House*, has the person stopped the abuse? The answer is "no."

It's like the alcoholic who gives up his favorite beverage, let's say it's beer, then switches to wine. Has he really given up his drinking? Or he switches from alcohol to drugs. Has he really quit? If somebody stops being physically abusive but continues to be verbally or emotionally abusive, is the person still abusive? All of the rooms in *The House* need to be emptied. That is no easy task.

A man may stop his physical abuse because he knows it could land him in jail. However, he continues to use one of the other kinds of abuse. He may even become more "skilled" at one of the other types of abuse. This shift in tactics is a common concern for women advocates who work with victims/survivors. The situation has changed, but not completely. The abuse continues.

Additional Rooms in The House

Sometimes people will extend *The House* metaphor, adding a basement, a roof, or a smoking chimney. Anything that captures the participants' attention is worthwhile.

THE BASEMENT

The basement room could include the "foundation" *The House* has been built on. Is the foundation built on love and trust, or anger and fear? What issues have caused "cracks" in the foundation? Major cracks may be caused by alcohol and drug abuse, crime, poverty, or other factors that place *The House* on unstable ground.

THE ROOF

A roof's main function is to protect a building's contents. However, the roof on this *House* could serve to keep things covered up or contained so as not to let them escape to the outside. The "secrets" are kept under cover.

Another overarching attribute is often placed on the roof of *The House*. The two words consistently used in discussing domestic abuse are *power* and *control*. These two words basically tell the story of why someone would abuse someone else. When assessing the rooms in *The House*, it should be clear that all these forms of abuse are ways someone will maintain power and control over someone else. In all abusive relationships these two factors exist.

The Men's Promise

When *The House* was completed, I asked the group: "How many grew up in a *House* like this one? What was the promise you made yourself?" Their common answer was, "I will never do that to my wife and kids!" My response in return: "Yet here you are, many years later, still denying this is happening in your *House*."

We make choices every day. A person chooses to abuse or not to abuse. Most men haven't really examined the shame of breaking this promise to themselves. Instead, most of their energy has been put into blame and denial. For many, this point in the discussion was a pivotal moment in recognizing they had broken their promise.

The House *Is Built*

Now *The House* has been built. Hopefully this exercise will offer readers a different look into the issue of violence in the home.

Remember the twelve-year-old boy at the beginning of the book? He successfully completed the group and became one of the positive forces to help other members confront their abuse. And his transformation was not an isolated experience in the men's treatment groups. Positive leaders emerge and play a critical role in the group process. This is the power of group treatment. There is nothing a counselor could say that would be more powerful than a fellow group member's positive voice.

It is now time to help the men look at the present day and their futures. The remaining weeks in the group focus on what steps to take to end their abuse.

CHAPTER SEVEN

Group Exercises
to End Abuse

This chapter examines a variety of exercises conducted in men's domestic abuse groups to provide them with the "tools" and "skills" to end their abuse. Men's domestic abuse programs throughout the country commonly use some of these skill-building exercises, and over the years our staff incorporated these standards as well as developing several exercises of our own.

I founded the men's program in 1981. The men's curriculum that members of the staff and I developed addresses the issue of men's domestic abuse in a thoughtful, compassionate, and respectful manner. It holds men accountable for their abusive behaviors and promotes the benefits of ending the abuse.

The men's curriculum is comprised of two books: *Foundations for Violence-Free Living: A Step-by Step Guide to Facilitating Men's Domestic Abuse Groups* and *On the Level: Foundations for Violence-Free Living*, a workbook that is given to each group participant.

Approaches to End Abuse

The following exercises involve a specific cognitive teaching approach. Some programs had men practice these skills in the group setting; other programs required written homework assignments to be completed outside the group sessions. The goal in all cases was to have men apply these new skills outside of group. Opinions about the effectiveness of these treatment approaches were mixed. I share my thoughts and experiences at the end of this chapter.

THE HOUSE OF ABUSE

The House is a primary example of an exercise to help men recognize the different kinds of abuse. Many men thought of abuse only as being physical. *The House* provides a more accurate definition of what constitutes abuse. This exercise offers a first step in helping men understand the impact of their abuse.

CUES

One common exercise was to identify a man's "cues" that signal he was getting increasingly upset. Each man would work to identify his specific cues. First, they were asked to identify their physical cues, things like muscles getting tight, clenching fists, or face and neck feeling hot. The women were very familiar with their partner's physical cues.

The second list of cues included situations or locations in which abuse was more likely to occur. Being under the influence of alcohol or drugs is a common predictor of abuse. Other identifiable situations that could trigger abusive behaviors might include holiday gatherings or being with certain friends or family members. Cues could include specific rooms in their home. Women identified the bedroom as a very volatile place where much of the abuse occurred.

A third list involved specific words or phrases that generated anger or hurt. "You're stupid." "You're a loser." "You're a drunk." "You're a worthless father." Such words could have a deeper meaning from the man's past than even their partners realized. They could trigger a return to his childhood experiences.

The fourth list of cues involved other "hot" subjects like parenting or household responsibilities. Money and sex are two major issues in most abusive relationships and often result in verbal, physical, or sexual abuse.

The men were asked to identify the feelings they were having during these critical moments. When asked to express these feelings the list usually consisted of four or five words: mad, angry, pissed-off, or bad. The men were given a "feeling word vocabulary" that lists over two hundred feeling words. The list is divided into five columns with the headings: happy/sad/confused/angry/scared. Each of the five columns contains roughly fifty words. Interestingly, the men knew almost all of the words and could identify that they had experienced most of them. The exercise involved the men talking about the times they thought it was anger they were feeling but it really could be something else, such as hurt, sad, unloved, inadequate, degraded, ashamed, rejected, humiliated, unappreciated, or helpless. The goal was to help the men identify other feelings that were behind what they thought was anger and learn how to express those in a different way.

TIME-OUT

Another common technique called "time-out" was taught as a method to prevent abuse. Most people are familiar with this sports and child-rearing reference. The technique taught to the men had several components, the primary goal of which was to physically leave the situation before any abuse happened. It is difficult to abuse someone if you are not in the same physical space. Ideally, the time-out would provide the man a "cool down" period in which he could find a better way to deal with the situation.

There were many problems with the time-out plan. On the surface it made sense, and if all parts of the time-out technique were followed, it could work. The primary problem was men wouldn't do it. They didn't leave and the abuse would occur, or if the men were successful at leaving the situation, when they returned it got worse. Instead of de-escalating, men would return fully equipped to make their case. Instead of cooling down, they heated up. Men found ways to misuse the time-out skill. They would call a time-out and use it as a way to go out with the guys or go drinking. Some even used it to go meet other women.

MOST VIOLENT INCIDENT

One exercise several programs conducted in men's groups, usually in a later group session, required participants to describe their "most violent incident." Each man would be given time—a half hour or more—to describe his most violent incident to the other group members. A great deal of group time was dedicated to this exercise. The purpose was to have men take responsibility for their abuse. After years of requiring this exercise as part of the program, we decided to discontinue it when we discovered that many men would use their time to attempt to tell their side of the story. In most cases it was not an accurate account of the incident. Men minimized, denied, and lied about their abuse. Even with the facilitator's best efforts, the exercise rarely produced the intended result.

Occasionally, a member gave a sincere account and took responsibility for the abuse. However, this success did not make up for the time wasted by other members who continued to avoid responsibility for their violence. Learning this lesson moved us to try a different strategy to help men take responsibility for their abuse.

TIME LINE

Eventually the "most violent incident" exercise was replaced with what was called a "time line." It involved each man telling the group about the "highs and lows" of his life, as far back as he could remember. A line would be drawn on a whiteboard, chalkboard, or large piece of paper displayed at the front of the group circle. The men would give a date when they could first remember a significant high or low in their life. Often it would go as far back as when they were five or six years old.

The facilitator helped direct the men with their time lines. This exercise was done in a later group session, after some trust had been achieved among the members. During a group session, two or three men presented their time lines. This exercise took several sessions for every member to complete the task, and for the most part, men shared more than expected. The men were genuinely interested and involved in this exercise. It allowed them to tell the story of their lives. Most had never done this before.

For lows, men listed events such as the divorce of their parents or a parent going to jail. School failures, being kicked off sports teams, or involvements with drugs, alcohol, or gangs were common lows. Men who were involved in criminal activities throughout their lives talked about the consequences they suffered. Other lows included failed intimate relationships, joblessness, poverty, and unmet childhood dreams. All, with rare exception, identified abuse in their childhood homes.

The highs included things like an achievement in sports or a significant relationship with a girlfriend, favorite coach, or adult mentor. For some men it was becoming a father or achieving sobriety.

The men reported far more lows than highs, the details of which were sobering. They shared many common experiences, especially with their lows. All of the dates were mapped out with the year and age of the member when these events occurred. Each man was required to do this exercise. Some were reluctant to participate, while others were enthused. One method that worked well was to have them draw a name from a hat to see who would go first and next.

THE MOST HURTFUL INCIDENT. The time lines ended at the present day. At this point the men would need to talk about the incident that brought them to the group. The "most violent incident" language was changed to "most hurtful incident" and seemed to help men be more truthful with their account of their abuse.

VICTIM EMPATHY. As a therapist facilitating the men's time lines, it was always difficult to view them as abusers and still have empathy and feel sadness for their pasts. The abuse in their childhood homes and the numerous failures in their young lives were monumental. One could predict a high likelihood that they would become abusive in their adult lives. The stories of their childhood and adolescence were a vivid reminder of what abuse does to its victims.

This exercise was not foolproof, but in our experience it was a good use of group time. It helped the men look at the abuse and how they suffered as childhood victims. It also helped them start to acknowledge their abuse as a perpetrator. One hope for this exercise was that it would help them begin to develop empathy for their intimate partners. Originally this exercise was presented in our adolescent groups. We then experimented with it in the men's groups and found it to be very effective. Our staff agreed this was one of the most powerful group experiences.

ANOTHER HIGH/LOW EXERCISE

At the beginning of each group session the men would take turns to identify their high and low for the past week. This icebreaker could be a quick check-in, or sometimes a significant event could have happened with one of the members. During these discussions the counselor might be made aware of a situation reported by a probation officer or a victim, for example a report of a violent incident or violation of a restraining order. The counselor would need to take into account the victim's safety and the confidentiality issues when deciding if, or how, to use this information. This exercise does not have to be done in every session depending upon time constraints, yet it can reveal some important current events.

CYCLE OF ABUSE

An exercise that was presented in the men's, women's, adolescent, and children's groups was called the "Cycle of Abuse." Lenore Walker's book *The Battered Woman* describes the cycle in great detail. The exercise began with a drawing on a board in front of the group. In the adult groups the drawing was a picture of a bell-shaped curve. A picture of a volcano was drawn for the adolescent and children's groups.

THE BUILDUP. The first phase of the cycle started at the lower left end of the curve or volcano. This was described as the "buildup" or "escalation" phase, when the person began to become irritated or angry. It could "simmer" for a while but continued to get hotter as the person moved up the curve. The facilitator reminded the men of their cues and that if they could recognize their cues, they might not reach the next phase of the curve.

THE EXPLOSION. The second phase of the curve was called the "blowup" or "explosion." This was typically where most abuse occurred.

THE HONEYMOON. The third phase was the "cool down." Some called it the "honeymoon" phase, where several things could happen. Women reported their partner would make promises such as "I will never do it again." Or he would buy gifts, candy, or flowers. Often, he wanted to have sex to ensure she had forgiven him.

WOMEN KNOW THE CYCLE. Women were very tuned in to the cycle of abuse. They were able to describe their own experiences and recognized the cycle and often tried to do things to interrupt its progression. Many said that initially the first two phases would occur followed by a honeymoon or makeup. But as the relationship deteriorated, women reported it was only the buildup and explosion phases over and over again. There was no remorse, no promise of not doing it again, only more abuse. The women's stories of how they had tried to deal with the man's cycle of abuse were many and diverse. Women talked about things they did to avoid or defuse the cycle in an effort to keep the abuse from happening. They became keenly aware of what must be done to keep themselves and their children safe.

MEN DESCRIBE THE CYCLE. I would ask the men if they thought the honeymoon phase was actually a honeymoon. After all, he had just exploded and abused her, now he wanted to have sex or expected forgiveness. For the most part, men agreed it was not a honeymoon.

Men often claimed that they would just "go off." They felt it happened without warning. They argued that they never saw the buildup but, instead, they would just explode. I asked, "How many things actually come out of the blue without any warning?" The men struggled to create such a list. I offered a couple of examples, such as an earthquake or a car accident. It could be argued that even in these examples there was a warning. If you live on a fault line, you are more likely to experience an earthquake. Many car accidents could be avoided if the driver wasn't distracted.

A group member might say that when he drank alcohol or was under the influence of drugs, he was not really himself, so he couldn't be held responsible. But his drinking or drug usage was a warning. If someone knows chemical use increases the chance of abuse, then that is a cue they learn to recognize. The purpose of showing this cycle of abuse is to debunk the excuse of men not seeing it coming.

HEALTHY AND UNHEALTHY RELATIONSHIPS

Another productive group exercise included making a list of what things made a healthy or unhealthy relationship. One half of the group would generate a list for healthy relationships. The other half of the group did the unhealthy list. Here are some of the actual items men came up with for both lists.

The healthy relationships list included: honesty, trust, communication, love, respect, understanding, sharing, compromise, joy, dedication, laughter, good sex, monogamy, emotional support, friends, family, loyalty, sympathetic, dependability, self-esteem, confidence, romance, compatibility, security, togetherness, faith.

The unhealthy relationships list included: drugs, alcohol, "no trust," cheating, lies, arguing, fighting, disrespect, lack of sex, controlling behavior, sarcasm, no empathy, affairs, money problems, no friends, bad sex, dishonesty, selfishness, low self-esteem, stealing, hardheadedness, laziness, unattractive appearance, lack of social life.

The two groups would then be brought back together to share their lists. It was encouraging to know men could identify what made a healthy or unhealthy relationship. The men would discuss these lists and take time to examine their past and present relationships. Most of them realized their relationships were unhealthy. The discussion also provided a look forward to future relationships and what behaviors they needed to change.

This was a helpful exercise to do in women's groups, as well as with adolescents and older children.

PROS AND CONS

A follow-up exercise to healthy and unhealthy relationships asks the question, "What are the pros and cons of abuse?" The men were asked to make a list of the pros or benefits of being abusive. It would take a moment for the men to respond. They hadn't considered anything positive about their abuse. They also created a list of cons. Usually, this list was longer.

The list of pros would include that a person would get their way. They would get what they wanted. They would win. Predictably, the list was short.

The lists of cons included that people get hurt or die. It made others afraid, or angry, or fight back. It produced turmoil, hate, and emotional scars. It caused relationship breakups and legal consequences.

Most people don't do things if there is no reward or benefit. When someone uses abuse, they are getting some benefit or reward from their behavior. The men knew the cons of abuse, but they hadn't consciously considered the pros.

A FATHER'S RELATIONSHIP

One exercise I developed addressed fatherhood. Not all of the men in the groups were fathers, but they all had a father. It was no surprise that fathers played a significant role in the men's lives. For many, their fathers were nonexistent. For others, the relationships were troubled and abusive. Occasionally a man claimed to have had a good father-and-son relationship. Sadly, these were very few.

The exercise consisted of a series of questions, including:

- What lessons did you learn from your father?
- On a 1–10 scale, how would you rate your relationship with your father?
- How would your children rate their relationship with you?
- In one word describe your father.
- What one word would your children use to describe you?

The men did this exercise in pairs and came back to the group to share their answers.

The relationships they described were telling. Men would talk about their memories and the struggles they had with their fathers. This discussion provided an easy lead-in to talking about their relationships with their children. For the men who were not fathers, it gave them some things to think about for the future.

THE PLAN

Toward the end of the sixteen-week group, I involved the men in an exercise to make a plan for their futures. I asked them to answer four fairly simple questions. If the man couldn't write, I would ask another group member to help him write or I would write for him.

These were the four questions:

1. What is the most important thing I have learned in the group?
2. What is my plan to end my abuse?
3. What tools will I use to prevent the abuse?
4. What will I miss about the group?

I had the men share their answers out loud. I reminded them of why they came into the group four months ago. I asked if they felt differently now versus back then. All were glad to be finished with the program, but there was a very different feel in the group, with much less hostility and defiance than the members had initially. They were able to talk with less blame and less focus on their partner's alleged abuse. Where there was once negative collusion, a positive sense of camaraderie had grown. Some men were able to develop friendships that appeared to be healthy and supportive.

Make no mistake: just because men completed the program and appeared to be more positive than when they started didn't mean they would end their abuse. I will address my version of "success" in the coming pages.

THERAPEUTIC EXERCISES
Meditation, relaxation practices, positive self-talk, physical exercise, one-word acronym techniques, assertiveness training, parenting skills, and family of origin were topics and exercises covered in men's groups. They focused on teaching men new skills to end their abuse. The important question is: do they work?

WRITTEN WORK
Some men's programs require lengthy written homework assignments, but this approach was unrealistic for the

majority of men referred to our men's groups. Most had very low reading and writing skills. Some could not read or write.

In my later work with men's groups, I had participants write on a piece of paper after each group session a response to the question, "What did you learn in the group tonight?" I emphasized they did not need to worry about spelling, but to write as best as they could. They needed to sign the paper and turn it in to me before they left the group or they would not get credit for the session. I saw firsthand the men's limited writing skills.

The men's responses to this one question provided valuable information. Some were able to repeat what happened in the session. Some were able to elaborate beyond a sentence with some insight. A couple times a man would write the word "nothing." It may have been an honest response. However, I made clear that if they learned nothing, the session would not count. I reminded them that the group was not a place to just do time. Jail was the place for those who wanted to do time.

Habilitation and Rehabilitation

There were times in the group the men reported they had an abusive incident. When asked if they recognized their cues or used one of their time-out skills, the answer often was "no." Some reported they did try to use one technique, but it didn't work. I explained that learning these new skills was like learning how to play a sport or an instrument. It would take practice and a lot of it. The difference was they had already learned and perfected the skill of abuse.

In thinking about learning new skills, two words come to mind: "habilitation" and "rehabilitation." The men have developed habits or have been "habilitated" on how to abuse. Most have years of experience and have become highly skilled at how to abuse someone. To "rehabilitate" or to learn and practice a new non-abusive skill was the goal.

I gave a couple of examples of how difficult it was to change a behavior. The first example was to ask who played a sport. Let's say you played football and you were a quarterback, or you were a baseball pitcher. You have always thrown the ball with your right hand. Now, you must only throw the ball with your left hand. How difficult would it be to get good at it? How easy would it be for you to go back to doing what you know best and throw with your right hand?

The same example could be applied to playing an instrument, like a guitar or piano. Imagine trying to switch your left and right hands, playing those notes the opposite way you learned and had done for years.

It's one thing if you want to learn how to do something new. But the reality was most of the men had no real interest in learning something new. They were comfortable with their current practices. Most of the men felt their abuse was justified or it didn't exist in the first place.

In large group trainings with general audiences, I sometimes asked the participants to do a simple exercise to show how difficult it is to change a behavior. I invited the audience members to switch jewelry, like a watch or a ring, to the opposite hand or wrist. What happened was interesting. Many refused to do it. If they did make the switch, within a very short period of time they would put the jewelry back to its original place. Everyone said it was uncomfortable and did not feel "right" or "normal."

Just think if you learned a behavior like "abuse." You practiced it for most of your life. How difficult would it be to change? For the men in the groups, abuse felt "right" or "normal." Even though most of the men agreed abuse was not right, it worked. They would win or get their way and basically have control or power over the person or situation.

To give up that power or control or "skill" would be to "lose." I told the men, "When you choose abuse, everybody loses. There are no winners."

Results

In my experience, these efforts to teach men new skills fell short, as the majority of the men did not put them into practice. Therefore, most often they were not effective. All of these newly taught skills could work only if the men consistently applied them. The problem was that very few did. Most went back to doing what was "natural." It was far easier to do what was familiar or ingrained. Many viewed other responses as weak or giving in. Their abusive responses worked, so why change? Men saw most of their situations with their partners as win/lose, and they were not willing to risk losing. The idea of giving men more "tools in their toolboxes" to solve problems sounded good. Unfortunately, most of the men still only pulled out the "hammer" to address the situation.

However, some men attempted to apply these new skills, and they worked. Some men stopped physically abusing their partners, mostly for fear of going to jail. They may have also become less abusive with their acts of verbal, emotional, or sexual abuse. However, less abuse was still abuse. The ultimate goal was to end all abuse, not to slow it down or reduce its occurrence. One might argue that less abuse could be considered a partial success. I know some programs would disagree with my conclusions, but only a very small percentage of men are successful at consistently applying these new skills in their relationships. My experiences in co-facilitating women's victims/survivors' groups confirmed much of what I believed to be true.

What Women Reported

Women who were in the victims/survivors' groups, whose partners were in the men's groups, reported mixed results regarding their partner's abusive behaviors. A few women identified some behavior change but questioned how long it would last. Others reported there was no change. Some said the physical abuse had stopped but other types of abuse had increased.

The majority of women in our women's groups did not have partners in the men's groups. These women hoped if they convinced their partners to attend the men's group, the men would end their abuse. Sadly, when these women heard the unsuccessful treatment stories, they were disheartened. However, this understanding provided them with a realistic view of the possible results of men's treatment.

Reflection

The end of the sixteen-week program was a time to reflect on the group experience. I asked the men to remember their first night in the group. They had interesting things to say about their memories of the early weeks in the group.

Men were anxious to leave, but many were visiting and talking about possibly seeing each other later on. I had them do one last exercise. I asked them to answer a familiar question, but this time to say it out loud to the group. We went around the circle, and each man said one thing they learned. I also had them identify one thing they would miss. Overall, they spoke positively about their time together. Even the most challenging group members seemed to have moved to a better place from where they came.

I remember one man who talked about his experience in the group. An atypical group member, he was an older, white, college-educated, middle-class owner of a successful business. He had a solid family life and successful marriage. Sadly, alcohol abuse became an issue and other kinds of abuse followed. He was one of the few men in the group who actually admitted to his abusive behaviors and expressed that he wanted to get help.

He reflected on his early days in the group, stating he felt he didn't have anything in common with the other members. The other men's hostility made him worry he would not get the help he was seeking. He said he had felt unsafe and didn't think he would continue in the group. He told the group he was amazed at how some of the angriest men in the group were able to change their original attitudes and negative outbursts. In the end, he felt the diversity of the men's life experiences shared in the group had opened his eyes to a whole new world. He felt he got the help he needed and even more.

I gave my closing comments. I thanked them for keeping their parachutes open and acknowledged their accomplishment of completing the group. For the last time, I told them their work was not over. Instead, completing group was just the first step in a lifetime of ending their abusive behaviors. Much like chemical dependency treatment for alcohol and drug abuse, there was not a one-time fix. It would involve an every minute, every hour, every day effort to live violence free. This unending effort was their only hope at ending abuse in *The House*.

I encouraged them to attend the men's aftercare group and seek out additional counseling to help them deal with their past and present abuse. The free aftercare group was in the same building and met weekly. It was available for anyone who had completed a men's group. After several years, the group was dissolved due to lack of attendance.

Chapter 12 addresses conclusions I have made as a result

of my experiences working with perpetrators and victims/ survivors of domestic violence. I respond to several frequently asked questions: "How successful are men at ending their abuse?" "Where do we invest our resources to end abuse in *The House*?" I also describe some lessons learned and what each one of us can do to help end this devastating problem in our homes.

CHAPTER EIGHT

The Women's Program

This chapter focuses on the women's program and addresses some of the issues female victims/survivors of domestic abuse face.

Helping Victims/Survivors

I would need to write a whole new book to fully describe my experiences in the women's groups. Instead, I will refer the reader to two books my colleague Kay-Laurel Fischer and I wrote in 1997.

The first, *Journey Beyond Abuse: A Step-by-Step Guide to Facilitating Women's Domestic Abuse Groups*, provides a curriculum for women's victims/survivors' groups. It offers exercises and techniques for facilitators of such groups. Therapists and others have used this book as part of their work with women. Staff at battered women's shelters have utilized these materials for their support groups. Women who are or have been involved in an abusive relationship or who know of someone who is also benefit from this book.

The second book, *Moving Beyond Abuse: Stories and Questions for Women Who Have Lived with Abuse*, was designed as a journal for participants in the women's groups. It tells their stories and their experiences in the group. It will be of interest to victims/survivors who want to hear other women's accounts of their abuse.

My experience as the only male in the women's victims/survivors' groups provided me with a deeper understanding of the issues women face in abusive relationships.

The women who participated in the victims/survivors' groups came voluntarily from numerous referral sources. Many were referred by community counseling agencies, battered women's shelters, private therapists, court intervention projects, child protection, family courts, and word of mouth. On rare occasions a woman would be court-ordered to attend the group. The majority of women were white. Some were college educated, from middle-class backgrounds, while others came from lower-income urban communities. A smaller number of women of color attended the groups, and nearly all felt the group experience met their needs. Women's groups specific to cultural and ethnic sensitivities were also available in the local neighborhood agencies that provided services for women of color.

The groups met for two and a half hours once a week for sixteen weeks. There would typically be eight to twelve women in each group and a female facilitator and sometimes a co-facilitator. (In the Clinician's Corner, I address facilitation of the group and changes we made as a result of our experiences.) The women's groups were conducted at the same site as the men's groups; however, they were on different days. The majority of the women attending the group did not have partners attending the men's groups.

The women's groups were a "support" group, designed for women who had been or were currently being abused to receive information and share their experience. In practice, it could also be considered a "therapy" group. The definition of what is support versus therapy is a fairly blurred line. The difference can be debated and actually become an issue. The program's primary philosophy emphasized an empowerment model to support women's decision-making process regarding their relationships. The group model was a key element that allowed women to gain strength and understanding from other women who shared similar experiences.

For more details about the content and structure of the women's groups, see the books cited above. In the next few pages, I address some of the most interesting and sometimes controversial issues of our women's program.

Why Do These Women Stay?

The question I have answered most often and in every setting is "Why do women stay?"

FLAWED QUESTION

Most people who ask this question are not familiar with the dynamics of domestic abuse. The question is flawed. The way the question should be asked is, "What *keeps* women in abusive relationships?" There is a major difference in the phrasing. The question "Why do women *stay* in abusive relationships" suggests *she* is doing something wrong. It subtly implies she might be to blame for staying in the abusive relationship. Possibly a person would view her as "weak." People who ask this question are questioning the woman's judgment. Many say they don't understand why she doesn't just leave. I often heard women say, "If a man did that to me just once, I would be out of there!"

One night in a men's session, a group member arrived very upset. Earlier that day he had been served with an order for protection or restraining order from the court. This court order restricted his contact with his partner and children.

The group members sided with the man and were equally upset, once again feeling the system was stacked against them. A member angrily blurted out, "Why do women stay?" I repeated the same question to the group.

The first three things the men said were: "Because they are stupid," "They must like it," and "It's not that bad!" I wrote these comments on the board. I then asked, "What could be some other reasons women might stay in an abusive relationship?"

It took some coaching, but the men did come up with a list. It included things like: She doesn't have any place else to go, or she doesn't want to leave the children. She has no money or no job, or her religious beliefs keep her from leaving. I would add, "Maybe she still loves you or she is hoping you will change." Many women talk about not wanting to end their relationships; they just want the abuse to stop.

Why Do Men Stay?

I would then ask the question of the men's group, "Why do men stay?" I pointed to the board at the first three reasons the men gave as to why women stayed: "Because they are stupid," "They must like it," or "It's not that bad!" If the men felt their partners had abused them, I suggested these might be the same reasons why they don't leave. This line of reasoning always got their attention. The men were uncomfortable with the revelation of how wrong their first three responses to their own question were.

I had the group members make a list of why men would stay in an abusive relationship. A few of the items were different from the women's list, but they were very similar. I pointed out that if they felt their partners were abusing them, they should consider why they are staying. When this question came up in the group, it produced an interesting exchange the men didn't expect. I often used this intervention exercise to address this question frequently asked by the men.

How Tough Is It to Leave?

A female colleague and I were asked to do training at a local hospital. The room was full of nurses, doctors, and other medical staff. The questions "Why do women stay?" and "How tough is it to leave?" eventually came up. My colleague, who had successfully left an abusive relationship, asked the female staff in the room: "How many of you could simply not return to your home tonight? You would have only the clothes on your back and the things in your purse. You may or may not be able to get your children. It could also mean that you might never return to that house again. How many of you could do it?"

The women in the room looked uncomfortable. These were professional women with good-paying jobs. They likely could financially support themselves and be independent of their partners. All of the women said it would be a very difficult decision. Most said they probably couldn't do it. It was an eye-opening experience for everyone in the room.

Women who are abused encounter numerous barriers to leave the relationship. Going to a shelter or packing up children to flee an abusive home is extremely difficult. Women also feel a stigma of what a battered woman looks like. Some women don't want to expose themselves or their abusive partner to their communities. The feelings of guilt and shame have a hold on many women who believe the falsehood that they have done something to cause the abuse. The decision to stay or leave an abusive relationship is incredibly complex. There are women who know their relationship is abusive and will choose to stay. Their reasons for staying vary, but it is their choice to make.

Women Who Leave

Studies indicate that women who leave their abusive partners will return, on average, seven times before they make a final break from their abuser. People ask, "Why does she return?" The list of reasons for not leaving is the same list for her to return.

Women would talk about their experiences of trying to leave their partners. It is one of the most dangerous times for her and the children. Making the decision to leave involves an incredible amount of emotional and physical energy. The fear of the unknown is something women think about when weighing whether to leave or to stay.

Another point women talked about related to their leaving or staying in the relationship: What other things happened as a result? For example, women reported a family member or friend telling her things that continue to instill self-doubt, such as, "You made your own bed; now lie in it." Sometimes a mother, sister, or friend who had been supportive of the woman leaving would give up out of frustration if the woman wouldn't leave or returned to her abuser. It is important for those well-intentioned and caring family members and friends to never give up.

The barriers to leaving an abusive relationship are overwhelming. It can be difficult for people who have never been in this situation to fully understand, but their continued support may someday help her get to a different place. They could help her succeed in getting free from the abuse or possibly even save her life. There are literally life and death decisions some women must make in these situations. In the women's groups, some have already left their abusive partners. Sometimes women in the groups would become frustrated with other group members who continued to stay in their abusive relationships. The counselor reminded them that each woman must make the decision to leave in her own time.

Overcoming Mistrust

Over the years, I had the privilege of working very closely with women in the Battered Women's Movement. In the beginning, I was viewed with a cautious and critical eye. I spent many hours with women advocates, program staff, and directors of women's programs, listening and talking out their concerns. The fact that I was a white, middle-class, college-educated, male professional held little credibility with the grassroots women pioneers who had spent years in the movement to help battered women. I had no experience and no standing. Besides, I was not asked to be at the table. Fortunately, over time, I was able to gain their trust and support and learned a great deal about domestic violence in the process.

A concern of battered women's programs was that men's counseling programs could be competing for funding for women's shelters and other support services for victims. Instead of taking away funding for victims, I was able to negotiate funds from the county's department of corrections for the women's victims/survivors' groups. At the time, corrections did not consider victims of abuse to be their responsibility. I made it a condition of our contract with corrections that our program would serve their domestic assault clients only if they provided funding for the victims.

During my years doing this work, I witnessed a dramatic change in opinions and in the system, mostly for the better. Different perspectives and knowledge provided everyone with a deeper understanding of the issues battered women face.

Shelter staff, court advocates, police, judges, lawyers, intervention programs, and others made up our team of participants. All of us spent many hours in meetings discussing how we would support each other's efforts and hold ourselves accountable in this difficult work.

Concerns About Counseling Victims/Survivors

I referred earlier to a serious issue that surfaced regarding providing counseling or "therapy" for women who were victims/survivors of domestic abuse. At the time, women who were active in the grassroots Battered Women's Movement had serious concerns about the label that might be applied to these victims/survivors. Some felt "therapy" or "counseling" for victims of domestic abuse would imply women were sick or had mental health issues. Others felt the professionals didn't understand victim issues and their clinical diagnosis would put the women at risk. Their abusive partners could possibly use these mental health diagnoses against the women in court.

There was mistrust of the professionals who were getting into the mix. Some felt the professionals were in it for their own financial interests. The reality for therapists who were serving this population was that in order to be paid for the therapy sessions, insurance companies required a mental health diagnosis. Some major conflicts arose between the two parties. The psychologists, social workers, and family therapists argued that women victims/survivors of domestic violence were suffering from such things as depression, anxiety, post-traumatic stress, or other mental health issues. But the grassroots advocates felt strongly that these diagnoses would be detrimental for the women. Both sides had valid arguments. The victims/survivors needed all the resources both groups provided.

I am not sure if this debate has been resolved or if it continues to be a point of contention. I know both groups agreed that as a result of the abuse women experienced significant physical and mental health concerns. The bottom line was that the varied services advocates and therapists provided were critical to the well-being of battered women and their children.

What About the Women?

A frequent question in the men's groups was "What about the women? My partner has abused me, and she doesn't have to go to a group. Why aren't women charged with abuse, only the men?" My first response was to remind the men: "No one deserves to be abused. If you feel you are being abused, you will need to make some decisions about what you are going to do. It may be that you will end the relationship. Or maybe go to counseling or get an order for protection from the courts. You do have choices if you feel you are a victim. Your partner will also need to decide what they will do." I would often be accused of taking the women's side. My response was: "I am on the side of ending abuse. I hope you will end up on that side too."

DO WOMEN ABUSE?

The question is "Are there women who abuse?" Again, the simple answer is "yes." A question I always pondered was: if these women had never been abused, would they have become abusive? That same question applied to the men. There are men and women who did not grow up in abusive homes yet became abusive in their own homes. There are also men and women who grew up in abusive homes who did not become abusive.

There is little doubt that children who grow up in abusive homes will be at risk for continuing the cycle of abuse in their adult lives. This recurring scenario was made obvious from the accounts of both the men and the women we served in our program. The "secret" of abuse in *The House* is still well hidden from public view. There is no question that females can be abusive and cause serious injury or even death to their intimate partners. Women have also been convicted of child abuse and neglect. These women should be subject to the same consequences as their male counterparts.

Who Is More Abusive?

Researchers who study domestic abuse have a difficult task. One early study was highly criticized for its methods and findings. It reported women were more abusive than men. The study interviewed men who had been abusive and women who had been abused. The question was: "Has the person been abusive toward their intimate partner?" When the researchers asked the men about their abusive behaviors, a majority of the men offered virtually no acknowledgment of their abuse. They were quick to report their partner's abuse toward them. When the women were asked the question, they said, "Yes, I have abused my partner." It was understandable how this flawed approach concluded women were more abusive than men.

In our women's victims/survivors' groups, women were quick to report they had been abusive toward their intimate male partners. They readily stated they had been verbally abusive, and some said they had become physically abusive as well. Women said they had slapped or pushed their partners. Some reported more serious incidents using objects or a weapon to hit or threaten. Women expressed their frustration with their partner's continuous abuse and claimed they had had enough and would fight back. They felt they needed to protect themselves from further harm. Some hoped that if they fought back he would stop his abuse. In many of these situations the women were acting in self-defense.

They would talk about other situations where they became abusive. It could be in retaliation for something their partner had done, for example seeing or calling other women. Some recalled that their physical abuse occurred when protecting their children from their partner's abuse. Most women were concerned and remorseful about their abusive behaviors. They worried about their children witnessing their abuse and the fear they saw in their children's faces when these abusive incidents happened.

The majority of men in the groups when asked if they were intimidated or feared grave harm from their partner's abuse responded, "no." They brushed it off as if it were not a serious concern. Occasionally men reported their partners would use an object like a frying pan or kitchen knife, but even those threats seemed not to generate much fear of bodily harm. Men agreed that in most situations their female partners were no match for them. In rare instances men did fear for their lives when a weapon was involved. On the other hand, women often reported that their partners used weapons to intimidate and cause physical injury. Again, I pondered, "If women were never abused by their intimate partners, would they have been abusive?" Once again, "No one deserves to be abused."

Research indicates there are women who perpetrate violence and there are male victims. However, women suffer far more injury and death due to domestic violence. They are also more impacted by the abuse, including suffering a greater amount of depression and other psychological problems. While the results show that both men and women experience abuse, the difference in the numbers is dramatic.

The National Coalition Against Domestic Violence

(NCADV), the Centers for Disease Control and Prevention (CDC), and other online resources provide valuable information related to domestic violence. A domestic abuse hotline can be accessed twenty-four hours a day. See resources, page 207.

As I told the men in the group: "Yes, women can be abusive, and they need to be held responsible for their abuse. There are no excuses for abuse." Women, like men, have grown up in violent homes and have experienced the same rooms in *The House*. The have also experienced the trauma and psychological scars.

I asked the men, "In your childhood home, who was the person that was abusive?" Almost always the men said it was their father. Rarely they identified their mother as the abuser. Sometimes men would say both. Most of the time when they identified their mother's abuse, it was her trying to defend herself from their father's behavior. Many felt their mothers were the victims and were no match for their fathers. Some men acknowledged their mothers had chemical abuse or possibly mental health issues, which they felt played a part in their abusive behaviors. They also reported their fathers seriously abused drugs and alcohol, which contributed to much of the violence. I asked the men if they ever tried to intervene to stop the abuse. Many men talked about how in their adolescence, when they were bigger and stronger, they would step in and try to protect their mothers from getting beaten.

The women in the groups talked about their son's behaviors. One minute he would be protecting them from his abusive father, and the next minute he would perpetrate abuse on them. This situation was distressing as well as confusing for the women. It created another fear that their son now was like his father. The thought of raising a son who would be abusive was deeply troubling.

How to Recognize an Abusive Relationship

There are several key signs that a relationship is unhealthy or abusive. Many women in the victims/survivors' groups talked about looking back in their dating relationships and early parts of their marriages where there were signs of abuse. Most ignored or didn't recognize these behaviors as abuse. They felt things would change or the behaviors weren't anything to be concerned about. Some of the abuse was subtle or not frequent enough to draw attention. Many women said they thought they could change their partner's behaviors or it would get better once they were married.

Jealousy and possessiveness were two of the most prominent signs women remembered. These examples held especially true in teenage relationships. Girls and young women thought this behavior was a sign of their partner's love and affection for them, even feeling flattered by his acts. Other predictors of abuse were his accusations and distrust of her and early signals of intimidation and anger. He might always want to know her whereabouts and which friends she was seeing, and he might display early signs of stalking and accusing her of cheating or telling frequent lies.

The women who had teenage daughters had already seen these signs with the boys their daughters were dating. Observing these behaviors was extremely concerning for the women, and they were fearful but felt helpless to affect the outcome.

The curriculum team for Planned Parenthood of the Southwest Ohio Region (https://www.plannedparenthood .org/planned-parenthood-southwest-ohio) published a checklist for recognizing unhealthy relationships. One mother said she gave her teenage daughter a copy of the questionnaire and shortly afterward the daughter broke up with her abusive boyfriend.

In our adolescent programs the teenage girls and boys answered the twelve yes or no questions about their dating relationships. Even if they were not dating, the list provided them with a look at the warning signs of an unhealthy or abusive relationship. When the women in the groups saw this checklist, many said that unfortunately they had not paid attention to the signs in their early dating relationships. They saw these behaviors in their adult relationships as well.

Here are the questions:

1. Does my boyfriend/girlfriend try to tell me what to do, how to dress, who to be with?

2. Do I spend most of my time worrying about our relationship?

3. Do I ever feel like he/she tries to make me mad on purpose?

4. Do I do more nice things for him/her than he/she does for me?

5. Does my girlfriend/boyfriend put unrealistic demands on me?

6. Does he/she ignore me or disrespect me when friends are around?

7. Have I quit doing things I used to enjoy since I've become involved with this person?

8. Does my boyfriend/girlfriend only act nice to me when he/she wants to have sex?

9. Has my girlfriend/boyfriend ever threatened or intimidated me?

10. Has my boyfriend/girlfriend ever said, "I can't live without you" or threatened to hurt themselves if I try to end the relationship?

11. Has my girlfriend/boyfriend ever physically harmed me?
12. Does my boyfriend/girlfriend insult me, put me down, or make me feel bad about my body or myself?

This exercise generated an interesting discussion with both the female and the male adolescents. They talked about their relationships as well as their friends' relationships. The amount of abuse that happens in these early dating relationships was eye-opening. The teens reported that in addition to the boys displaying many if not all of these abusive actions, some girls exhibited similar behaviors.

There's a Man in the Group

A number of issues surfaced during the program's early years regarding the ideal staffing of the men's and women's victims/survivors' groups. One of the most controversial issues we confronted was something none of us had considered initially as we facilitated the groups. For many years our program's female staff facilitated the women's victims/survivors' groups and the male staff facilitated the men's groups. The practice of having only female staff facilitate women's groups and male staff facilitate men's groups was the norm in domestic abuse programs across the country. In the beginning of the program, only two of us facilitated all of the groups. As the number of staff grew and more groups were added, the practice of men facilitating the men's groups and women facilitating the women's groups continued.

After many years of facilitating groups in this manner and months of discussion, we decided to have male staff co-facilitate women's groups with a female therapist as well as female staff co-facilitate men's groups with a male therapist. This change became a powerful experience for the staff and participants alike. The Clinician's Corner appendix details the decision-making process and the results of this change in our treatment approach.

Prior to when I co-facilitated the sixteen-week women's groups, I would be invited as a guest speaker in these groups. I was given a list of questions the women wanted answered, including what impact the abuse would have on the children and whether the men really change. Many women shared their specific concerns and wanted to know my thoughts. I made it clear I did not have all the answers. I could only offer them my experiences from the men's groups.

One woman described her teenage son protecting her from her partner's physical assaults. Later, her son would verbally abuse her like his father and at times even become physical. She felt confused and frightened by his contradictory behavior. She worried what his future relationships with women would be like. Other women shared similar experiences. Some reported their partners were less abusive, but they were waiting for the "other shoe to drop." They would ask me, "How do I know if he has really changed?" My best answer was "Trust your gut!" Far better than anyone, they know their partner's abusive signs and behaviors from their past experiences. He may be "white knuckling" his behavior in the short term, but they need to pay attention to his long-term actions.

I didn't want to be the bearer of bad news, but I wanted to be truthful. I told them that in my experience very few men would do the work to end their abuse, but I felt it was important to also say it is possible for some men to change. I made it clear there is no "magic treatment" for their partners.

I could write about many insights from being the only male in a women's victims/survivors' group. The most important was finding out the women's experiences of having a male present. At the start of group and in their initial intake, the women were asked to voice their concerns about having a male co-facilitator. The response was mixed, but the majority of the women were willing to accept the arrangement.

At the end of the sixteen weeks, the women reflected on their initial apprehensions regarding having a man in group. They had been concerned about how safe it would be to talk about the abuse from their male partners. The mistrust and fear they had for men was understandable. In the end, the women felt the experience was overwhelmingly positive. Having a "healthy male" listen and acknowledge their experiences was validating and very beneficial. The vast majority felt the positives far outweighed the negatives. They said we should continue with this male/female co-leadership approach.

A word of caution regarding male co-facilitators in women's victims/survivors' groups: it can be disastrous. It has to be the right male and female team or it will be detrimental for the participants. Having female co-leaders in men's groups was another debatable decision that resulted in some remarkable outcomes. See more on this practice in appendix 1.

Life After Group

For many years women would report back to us how their lives had changed. This ongoing connection was in sharp contrast to the men, whom we rarely heard from after their group ended. For some women, it took a long time to end their abusive relationships. For others, it was immediate. Unfortunately, some became involved in another abusive relationship. The good news was that they were able to recognize the abuse much sooner than in the past and end these relationships.

My experiences in co-facilitating the sixteen-week women's groups gave me hope for their lives and for their children's lives to become free from abuse. They were receiving the support they needed to make a decision to stay or leave their abusive relationships. Although the road might not be easy, I watched the women make changes that possibly never would have occurred if they hadn't received the support and information from the women's groups. The stark differences between the men's progress versus the women's progress was notable. Sadly, the men spent much of their time denying and blaming, while the women spent their time supporting and growing. I viewed the men as taking baby steps toward change compared to the women taking giant leaps.

While fairy tale endings were few and far between, many women felt their lives were dramatically better. Some women said the group literally saved their life. Most of the women felt the group experience gave them what they needed to make informed decisions about their intimate relationships. Upon completion of the group, many reported they did not want the connection to end. They were worried what they would do without the group support.

A women's aftercare support group was formed. Interestingly, only a small percentage of the women continued. Those who did typically attended for a short period of time. Women reported they didn't have the same bond in the aftercare group as they had with the women in their original group. A few became long-term attendees who relied on the other women's support, and the group became an important part of their lives. The aftercare group continued for many years, and women would come and go as they felt the need.

I could report much more on the women's struggles and their experiences in the groups. For a more detailed account of the women's program, please refer to the two books listed at the beginning of this chapter.

CHAPTER NINE

Couples Counseling

This chapter addresses the subject of couples counseling as a treatment method when domestic abuse is present.

Drawbacks to Couples Counseling

Several women who sought help in our program reported they had previously participated in couples or marriage counseling with their partners. Their experiences varied, but most said it was not helpful. Women revealed that many therapists never asked about the abuse. The focus was on communicating better and addressing other issues but not specifically on the abuse. They reported that often the only way their male partner agreed to participate in counseling was if he could choose the therapist, usually a male. Some women reported they felt the therapist sided with the man regardless of whether the therapist was male or female. Women said their partners would act calm and even charming if the therapist was a woman.

In other counseling experiences the therapists did address the abuse and held the man accountable. In most cases, if the man believed the therapist favored the woman, he would refuse to continue counseling. Sometimes the woman would continue with the therapy and address the abuse. Many private therapists would refer the women to our women's groups for additional support. Women often described the counseling they received in women's groups as far more beneficial than their prior couples counseling experiences.

In the 1980s, several domestic abuse treatment programs were starting up throughout the country. Debates began to surface over what treatment model would best serve perpetrators and the victims/survivors of domestic abuse. There were strong opinions that couples counseling was inappropriate for victims/survivors of domestic abuse. In fact, most believed it could be potentially dangerous for the victims. This was also our position. There was no known research to determine if this opinion was valid. However, the stories from countless victims/survivors were enough to support our conclusions.

Military Couples Treatment Program

One program implemented throughout the Marine Corps and Navy was a couples counseling treatment model. This particular program, in place at numerous bases in the United States and abroad, was designed to serve married couples who were on active duty serving in the military. Its primary treatment approach was to provide groups for couples where domestic abuse had been reported.

Civilian law enforcement or military police would respond to a domestic incident and make an arrest. The case would be reported to the service member's command. He would be charged with domestic assault and ordered by his command to attend the couples treatment group. The female spouses were not mandated to attend but were strongly encouraged to participate. Typically, the male participants were young married enlisted marines and sailors who lived in base housing or in the surrounding civilian communities. Most were from the lower military ranks. Only a few participants were older and more senior in rank.

In the mid-'80s the Navy asked me to present our treatment model and its rationale. I had a unique perspective: in addition to my civilian work with perpetrators and victims/survivors, I was a member of the Naval Reserves. I also had served as both an enlisted member and an officer. I was invited to speak to government services clinicians and uniformed Navy social workers who were providing the couples counseling groups. They had many questions as to why I thought the couples treatment model was not appropriate for serving both the perpetrators and the victims of their domestic assault cases. I developed a story to help explain why I was opposed to the Navy and Marine Corps couples counseling method of treatment.

The Pilot Story

"Let's pretend I am a Navy or Marine pilot and you are a female prisoner of war. One day I fly into the prisoner of war camp and I am able to rescue you from your captors. I know that you have been abused and probably tortured by your captors, but I am here now and your captors will need to answer for their abusive actions. I want you to tell me everything they have done to you over these past months or years of your captivity. Tell me all these things in front of your captors so that they can hear what they have done. Oh, one more thing: I have to leave in an hour, and you have to find your own way out of here."

I posed a question to the clinicians in the audience: "If you were the woman prisoner, how much do you think you should say about the abuse and torture you experienced?" The clinicians got the picture. In my view, the couples counseling approach with victims of domestic abuse puts the woman in the exact position as the woman prisoner in this scenario. Her safety would be in jeopardy. In fact, the situation could be lethal.

Still, not everyone was convinced couples counseling should be discarded as the treatment model. I asked another question of the counselors facilitating the couples' groups: "How many of the women dropped out of the groups?" Their answers revealed a significantly high dropout rate among the women in the couples' groups. In many cases there was no follow-up with them to check on their concerns or safety. By contrast, very few women in our women's groups failed to continue in the group. I offered one last comment: "If you really want to find out how successful a couples counseling session is, place a hidden tape recorder in the back seat of the car. The recording of the ride home could tell you a lot!"

Women in our groups told horrendous stories of the rides home from their previous couples counseling sessions. They described serious arguments and assaults, even being shoved out of a moving vehicle and left to walk home. If the abuse didn't happen during the car ride, it often occurred in the privacy of their home. The women recounted verbal, physical, and sexual abuse after the couples counseling sessions.

The majority of women attending our groups did so without their partner's knowledge. They feared his response and the possibility he would sabotage their efforts to get help. It was difficult for women who were still with their abusive partners to return home after a women's group. They felt torn with their decision to stay or leave and reflected on what was discussed in the group. It was different when their partner was not in the counseling session and was unaware of her attendance or what transpired. Women reported that if their partners did learn of their counseling outing, the partners would question them on what happened in their "men's bashing" group.

What Happened with the Navy's Couples' Groups?

In the end the Navy reexamined its counseling programs and adopted much of what our program offered. It was not that we had the right or only answer, but our approach increased their awareness of what could be another treatment model, especially given the real risks victims could possibly face.

Appendix 2 details the differences in addressing the issue of domestic abuse in the military versus within the civilian population.

The Couples Experiment

A small number of participants in our women's groups approached their group therapists and asked if we would consider offering a couples' group. Their partners were participants in our men's groups, and the women reported some positive changes in their partners' behaviors. They hoped that given the right kind of counseling, their relationship with their abusive partner might be salvaged. After much discussion and drawing on many years of experience in providing separate counseling groups for the men and women in our programs, we decided to honor their request. Although we were highly skeptical of the outcome, we felt we were the best prepared to provide this service.

Our women's and men's therapists determined the criteria for the couples' group. First, each person had to have successfully completed their separate men's or women's group. The couple would need approval from their respective group counselors to attend the couples' group. Second, the couple had to confirm the abuse had stopped, and both parties acknowledged neither was being coerced to participate in the counseling. A final condition was the couple's intention to continue in their relationship. It was not an "uncoupling" group. The group would be co-facilitated by a female and a male therapist from our program.

What Happened Next?

Unfortunately, the majority of the couples never finished the process. The men struggled with taking responsibility for their abuse and often regressed to their old behaviors of blaming their partners. This attitude was very disheartening for the men's groups' counselors, as these men were perceived to have made the most progress to end their abuse.

The women in the couples' group talked about their hopes of continuing their relationship. But most of the women ended up realizing that the relationship needed to end. The women experienced grief and loss, but also felt a sense of closure and some relief. For most of the women it had been a long, tough road that finally seemed to be coming to an end. Many of the women continued to participate in the women's aftercare support group. There they were able to work toward putting the abuse behind them and healing from the trauma it had caused. Many also enrolled their children in the children's groups to help them deal with the impact the abuse had on their young lives.

The Very Few

A small number of couples in the group did manage to continue in their relationships. It wasn't clear if these couples would find long-term success. The counseling staff felt they had provided the information and the tools for the couples to live without abuse. The rest would be up to them.

After a few years of providing the couples' group, we determined it was not the best use of our limited staff resources. The experiment provided us with firsthand experience as to the pros and cons of couples counseling with perpetrators and victims/survivors of domestic abuse. Although in most cases the women did not reach their initial objective of salvaging their relationships, they could feel some comfort in having done everything possible to save them.

CHAPTER TEN

Chemical Abuse and Domestic Violence

This chapter explores the issue of chemical use and abuse as it relates to domestic violence.

A Simple Definition

One day a very good friend approached me with concerns regarding his partner's alcohol use. He was distraught and frustrated with her behavior when she had been drinking. He described her as a different person. But he wasn't really sure if she had a problem with drinking and wanted to know how he could tell. He would drink socially with her and felt he managed his alcohol consumption responsibly. On occasion he had confronted her when she got drunk, but it only led to an argument, and she would point out his drinking.

I shared with him my very simple definition for determining if a person has a drug or alcohol problem: "If alcohol or drugs are causing a problem in their life or the lives of others around them, it's a problem. If the person is losing a job, a driver's license, a relationship, or their freedom, it's a problem. Or if it's causing repeated fights and arguments and abuse of others, it might be time to stop drinking or using drugs." The real problem is how to tell or convince someone else they have a problem with chemical abuse. My friend had tried to tell his partner multiple times that she should look at her drinking, but he got the "stiff arm" to the face.

Over 70 percent of the men in the domestic abuse groups had alcohol and drug issues. I would ask them to think about who in their lives told them they had a chemical problem. Was it a stranger on the street? Was it their drinking or drug-using buddies? No, it was their intimate partner, a child, a good friend, a family member, or maybe even an employer. These were the usual messengers, because they were the ones who had been hurt by the user's behavior. More importantly, these were the ones who loved or cared about the user and wanted them to get help. No stranger or drinking/drug buddy is going to risk the wrath of confronting someone's chemical use. It's loved ones who take that risk. They are the ones who have firsthand experience and are invested in the person's well-being.

Sadly, these are the ones who get the anger directed at them and suffer verbal or even physical attacks. They are also the ones blamed for the abuser's problem. Unfortunately, after a certain period of time, many of these concerned loved ones give up on their efforts to help. Can you blame them? They are tired and feel hopeless.

Confronting an individual's chemical use or abuse is one of the most difficult interventions a person can make. One chemical dependency counselor commented that she believed addressing a mother with her chemical abuse is even tougher than confronting a father. Mothers hold a special place in the family, which can make it harder to intervene. Resources are available to help with this challenging undertaking of dealing with someone's chemical abuse. It is not easy, but if the intervention is successful, it will be well worth the effort.

Chemical Dependency Programs and Domestic Abuse

In the early 1980s, there were many drug and alcohol treatment programs in the area where I worked. I was asked to do training with several chemical dependency (CD) treatment programs' staff on the topic of domestic abuse. At the time, this subject was not discussed much in CD treatment. These counselors had their work cut out for them just trying to get folks sober.

I introduced *The House* exercise, and we discussed the issue of alcohol and drugs as a contributing factor. I made the following point, which always surprised the CD treatment staff: all alcoholics and addicts are also domestic abusers, but not all domestic abusers are alcoholics or addicts. There would be some puzzled looks on their faces. I confirmed the statement by saying that at a bare minimum, people with drug or alcohol problems were emotionally abusive in their relationships. Anyone who has lived in a home where alcohol or drug abuse is an issue knows emotional abuse occurs. Other kinds of abuse—verbal, physical, and sexual—are likely to be present as well. The task of helping people end their chemical use in addition to their domestic abuse left the CD counselors feeling overwhelmed.

Sobriety and Abuse

I told them about a man in a group who said he had eight years of sobriety, but his domestic abuse continued. He realized after coming to the group that he was still verbally and emotionally abusive toward his wife. He was very aware of his issue and wanted to change in an effort to keep his marriage, which was on the verge of ending. He was more aware of his problem than most of the other group members. I attributed his insights into his abusive behavior to his long-term sobriety and involvement with Alcoholics Anonymous.

Difficult to Measure

I also talked with the CD staff about a practice that recognizes a participant's length of sobriety. Usually, the person earns a medallion or pin that signifies a milestone of being chemically free. Most of the time the person has a specific date or place he or she could identify as the last time they used alcohol or drugs. I explained that identifying a specific date or time when a person ended *all* forms of domestic abuse was not going to be easy. Maybe the person could identify the last time they were physically or sexually abusive, but what about the last time they were verbally or emotionally abusive?

The strength and effort it takes to end alcohol or drug abuse is massive. To add the challenge of ending *all* forms of domestic abuse feels almost impossible. Not many of the men in the domestic abuse groups were ready to give up their alcohol and drugs, just as most were not ready to change their abusive behaviors. Ending their alcohol and drug abuse wouldn't guarantee their other abusive behaviors would cease, but it would be a start.

Which Comes First?

Opinions were mixed regarding the need for men to be chemically free before they were allowed to participate in a domestic abuse group. In a perfect world, prior to participating in a men's domestic abuse group, a person would be required to have extended sobriety and also be involved in a chemical dependency support group. Some of the men in our groups were attending CD treatment or outpatient aftercare support groups. Others were required to attend a CD program after completing the domestic abuse group. Still others had no requirement to receive CD treatment.

Because chemical abuse plays such a significant role in many domestic abuse cases, it makes sense to address this issue first. For the majority of men referred to our program this was not a viable option, mainly because of the overwhelming number of domestic assault court cases and the costs. Monitoring the men's chemical use outside of the group would require a great deal of effort and resources that weren't available for most programs. If abstinence from chemicals was part of the court order, a probation officer would be responsible for monitoring the probationer's compliance with the court mandate.

Does it make sense to provide domestic abuse counseling to men who are still using alcohol or drugs? I knew it was not the ideal approach, but given the options, addressing their domestic abuse was still better than doing nothing. Waiting for someone to get sober or drug free might mean the counseling would never begin.

One benefit of having the men participate in the domestic abuse groups prior to CD treatment was they heard from other men who were sober or working on their sobriety, like the man who had been sober for eight years. He spoke positively about his CD treatment experiences and life free from alcohol and drugs. Some members who were recovering would confront the men who were still using and encourage them to get help. Not everyone shared the same views, and some unhelpful perspectives would be addressed. I did infrequently witness men in the domestic abuse groups become more amenable to the idea of CD treatment in the future. The Clinician's Corner appendix addresses the rules regarding chemical use as it applied to participation in the men's domestic abuse groups.

More About Alcohol, Drugs, and Domestic Abuse

In a society where alcohol use is legal and is a widely acceptable form of recreation, it is hard to be the one who can't participate. Sobriety makes you an outsider, perhaps even viewed as "weak" or "pathetic." Drug use has its own history, and a status that is constantly changing. The verdict is still out as to how the American public will view those who use drugs, especially the ones that provide a form of "recreation."

Everyone who reads this book likely knows someone who has or has had an alcohol or drug problem. It wasn't that long ago that many thought only skid row street people were the "drunks.'" It shocked many of us to find out they were also our parents, the minister, Aunt Mabel, Uncle Eddy, our siblings, a friend, the favorite fifth-grade teacher, or the family doctor. It took a while to change our attitudes and increase our understanding of this deadly disease.

As for drug abuse, the view held by many was that only minorities or lower-class whites had a problem. But we've learned that drug addiction occurs in all populations regardless of race, age, or social status. Our views on drug and alcohol use and abuse are varied, and our solutions to end the abuse do not always work. Yet we need to keep trying to help those who need it.

The same holds true for those impacted by domestic violence. We need to keep examining our assumptions of and attitudes toward the victims and perpetrators of domestic abuse. It starts with an increased awareness and a collective effort to continue to find ways to address what goes on in *The House.*

One Last Word

I told the men's group that the problem with drug and alcohol abuse was that, in most cases, it didn't kill you right away. It could be a very "slow death." It also forced those around them to have a painfully slow and unpleasant experience. Those who grew up in an alcoholic or drug-dependent *House* understood that point vividly. The anxiety and fear that children and adolescents experienced as a result of a parent or adult caretaker's chemical abuse was enormous. I would remind them of their time lines, where the majority reported the chemical abuse in their homes contributed to destroying their families. Most of the men were still denying their own chemical abuse, and yet they knew the damage it caused to themselves and others. I acknowledged the men in the group who had taken steps to end their chemical use. I commended them on their strength and courage to make this change in their lives. Relatively few people successfully end their chemical abuse. Those who are successful deserve all the credit and respect for their achievement of this seemingly unreachable goal.

Helping those who were still actively using and abusing chemicals end their abusive behaviors was not an easy task. It might even be unrealistic. Yet I believe participating in a treatment or support group of any kind could open a person's mind to other options. Most of the men who had participated in a CD treatment program prior to the domestic abuse group were much more open to the idea of ending their violence. The same could be true with a reverse order of treatment. In the end, if men don't get help with ending their chemical and domestic abuse, their lives and the lives of those around them will be dismal.

CHAPTER ELEVEN

Other Programs

This chapter briefly describes other programs our staff developed and implemented during the three decades our program was in existence. These programs served the specific needs of individuals in the community. The men's and women's domestic abuse groups helped us determine other unmet needs in our schools and correctional programs serving adolescents and adults.

The Children's Programs

Shortly after the men's and women's domestic abuse programs were started, it was obvious that we should develop a children's program. The women in the victims/survivors' groups expressed concerns regarding the impact the abuse by their intimate partners was having on their children.

Our staff developed and implemented a group therapy program for children ages four to twelve. The groups were divided into mixed gender, age-appropriate cohorts (ages 4–6, 7–9, and 10–12). The groups met once per week in the same facility as the women's groups.

The groups were ninety minutes in length and were

usually co-facilitated by a female and a male counselor. The mothers would meet in another room in a parenting support group and discuss different topics related to the impact of abuse on the children.

The children's groups were designed to have the children talk about their feelings and address the abuse in a way that helped them feel safe and supported. The staff developed many exercises and activities to help the children express their feelings and concerns. Play therapy, art projects, and games were all age appropriate to support the children in their group experience. Addressing the abuse so that the children could talk about it was crucial, although it was remarkable how many of the children could openly discuss their experiences and fears.

As one can imagine, these children had experienced and still were experiencing the trauma described in the previous chapters. It was troubling to think how many of them would be returning to their homes after the group and be back in the rooms where it happens.

The groups involved a lot of sitting on the floor and ups and downs for the children and the group leaders alike. The highlight was always the long-anticipated snack time at the end of each session.

These children's groups were amazing. The children loved the groups and their connection with the therapists. Many wanted to continue past the twelve-week program. Some returned and moved into the next age group when they were eligible. Some families were involved in the groups for over a year. The mothers, and an occasional father, who participated in the parenting group were given new ways to support their children and help them navigate the issues the abuse had caused in their lives. At a minimum, the children's groups provided an early positive counseling experience. These children will continue to need help and support later on, but hopefully this early encounter with counseling will make it more palatable for them to seek help.

The fathers who were participants in the men's program could also attend the parenting group and involve their children in the children's groups. It was rare that any of the fathers enrolled themselves or their children in the groups. Given our concerns with couples counseling (see chapter 9), couples were not allowed to attend the parenting support group. Some issues surfaced with the few men who attended the parenting group—for example, making advances at women in the group, dominating the group time, or other inappropriate behaviors. Immediate action was taken to address the problem.

There were many barriers to providing these children's groups. Although there was no cost for the service, many women were without transportation and other resources and thus prevented from getting needed help. In several cases, our counseling staff went to the homes or even the schools and picked up the mothers and their children to take them to and from the groups.

Another obstacle was that some men who had shared custody of their children prohibited the children from attending the groups. Court hearings, custody battles, and attorney involvements were some of the constant issues many of the women had to overcome to get help for their children. The men also felt they were victims of the same court fights and costs that plagued the women.

Many articles and books describe the impact that abuse has on children. Participants in the parenting group benefited from this information, including warning signs of behaviors children can exhibit. All children react differently to abuse. One of the most important messages from the therapists who facilitated the children's groups was to let the children know the abuse is not their fault.

Warning Signs of Abuse

Warning signs might include a change in the child's (or adolescent's) behavior. There could be noticeable changes at school, such as failing grades, trouble with peers or teachers, withdrawal or isolation from friends or activities, gang involvement, and looking depressed or sad. There could be physical signs, like headaches, stomach issues, mood swings, or weight loss or gain. The signs of eating disorder, drug or alcohol use or abuse, and suicidal thoughts are all serious concerns. Any changes in a child's behaviors could point to trouble in their lives, not only abuse in the home but being bullied in school. The next section describes an anti-bullying program implemented in several middle schools.

High-achieving children who appear to be successful at school but who are experiencing violence in their homes are more challenging to recognize. These may be the top scholars in their class, the star athletes, the "pleasers" who look and act just fine but are struggling with anxiety, depression, or other mental and physical health issues with no visible signs. Children are resilient, but if the issues go untreated, other serious problems could occur. Drug and alcohol abuse, suicide, gang involvement, dropping out of school, or criminal behavior are all issues children and adolescents who have been abused can suffer.

Our limited resources to end abuse should focus on the children, including adolescents. The children's domestic abuse groups provided the children and their parents with an opportunity to begin to identify and attend to their needs. The challenges are many, but the rewards are great.

It can't be overstated that teachers, coaches, clergy, youth leaders, aunts, uncles, grandparents, neighbors, or friends can be influential in helping a child in need. It doesn't have to be a parent, and sometimes it shouldn't be the parent, who fulfills this role. Think about the people in your life who made a difference. My guess is this list includes someone who was not your parent.

Cool 2B Safe

In the early 1990s, a colleague and I developed and implemented an anti-bullying program called Cool 2B Safe. This school-based program was designed to work with middle school children, grades six through eight. It was modeled after the Olweus Bullying Prevention Program (OBPP) in Norway.*

The program's primary goal was to reduce and prevent bullying by establishing a school climate that was supported throughout the school. It involved the entire student body and included buy-in from the principal on down. All faculty, administrators, and custodial staff were required to attend the ongoing trainings. We expected the school staff to be involved at various levels in carrying out and supporting the program's strategies and goals.

Originally the focus was on one inner-city middle school; later it was expanded to other middle schools in the area. The student population consisted of African American, White, Hmong, Latino, Native American, Somali, and other cultural and ethnic groups, primarily from low-income families. Several students were English language learners and many of them had non-English-speaking parents. The core of the Cool 2B Safe program was based on the OBPP model;

---

*For more information about this program and ending bullying in schools, seek out information about Dr. Dan Olweus's program (for example, https://olweus.sites.clemson.edu/). His approach has been expanded in the United States. We produced a Cool 2B Safe curriculum and video, which does not seem to be available online but may be in some library collections.

however, we adapted it to meet the diverse needs of the student body, a much different population than that served in Norway. Our staff reflected the diversity of some of the students, which was a critical factor in reaching the different student groups.

The program was established to develop a climate that engaged everyone in creating a safe and violence-free school, where bullying behavior would not be tolerated and would be appropriately addressed. Our staff worked with specific groups of students and facilitated various activities and projects that involved team building, cooperative learning, and positive conflict resolution, all focusing on student roles in preventing and eliminating bullying and violence in the school. Our staff were invited to participate in the classroom setting to assist teachers with presenting the information to the students. It was important to show the students that the teachers and our staff were working together to support the messages of anti-bullying.

This program could succeed only if the school principal was in support of the project. Fortunately, the principals in the schools we served were totally on board. The teachers and other school staff were also key to carrying out the program's goals. I worked with some incredible teachers, and as I observed them in their classrooms, I developed a deep appreciation for their skills and talents.

Ultimately the students themselves had to do the work. They were the ones who were being bullied, witnessing the bullying, or doing the bullying. Sometimes it was all three. I saw many examples in the hallways, classrooms, gyms, playgrounds, and lunchrooms where bullies found their victims. The adults in the building needed to know they have a key role in recognizing and confronting this problem. Bullying has existed in schools forever and is still present today. I know some school staff may not view this monitoring as part of their job, but if they don't make an effort to stop it, who will? Our staff worked with the students to talk about the role of "bystanders"—those who stand by and watch or possibly even encourage the bullying. Teaching students what actions they can take to stop the bullying in their school is a powerful tool. They all know who does the bullying; it's important they know the options and the role they can play.

At one of the schools in our program, two girls got into a fight. One had a box cutter razorblade knife and slashed the other's throat. It was a horrible scene. Many students and faculty witnessed the bloody scenario and were deeply disturbed by it. Thankfully, the girl survived.

Our staff were called to the scene to de-escalate the situation and provide counseling for the students. Apparently, the incident may have been somewhat gang related. There was talk of retaliation by the friends of the girl who was injured. Because of our relationships with the students, built through the Cool 2B Safe project, we were able to intervene and work to prevent any more violence. The faculty, the administrators, and our staff worked closely with the students. The students played a critical role by talking with their peers, and no further violence occurred.

One might already see the connection between this anti-bullying work and domestic violence. Many participants in the men's groups were bullies in their schools. They used their power to abuse and control their victims. Years later, they "bullied" their intimate partners. *Bullying* is a watered-down word for abuse. Bullies abuse their victims. They intimidate and torture and assault their victims. Taking someone's lunch money or food as a child is replaced by actions against an intimate partner as an adult. Much bullying behavior in school has gone unchecked. By turning a blind eye, we give permission for the behavior to continue. If we want to send the message that these behaviors are not acceptable and will not be tolerated, our work needs to start in the schools. School staff could argue that the work needs to start in the home. That is true, but if these children are living in *The House*, the problem most likely isn't going to be handled there.

School Suspension Program

Our staff also developed a School Suspension Program (SSP), designed to provide a place for middle school students who were suspended for one to three days to receive help with their acting-out behaviors at school. Prior to this program being offered to the school, students were sent home for the duration of the suspension. Often the students were sent to an unsupervised setting, where they could run free and continue to fall behind in their studies. To most people, this practice didn't make any sense.

In our program, the students were sent to an alternative site, where our staff provided a full day of supervision and aid to these students. The day began with the students meeting our program staff outside of their school (the students were not allowed inside). A special bus took them to the alternative site. Staff rode the bus with the students and addressed any issues that occurred during transport. They would also start building relationships with the students and preparing them for the day ahead.

At the alternative site, the students worked on their missed assignments and received individual tutoring from our counseling staff. They also spent time discussing the events and behaviors that led to their suspensions. The counseling staff conducted conflict resolution exercises and facilitated discussions focusing on behavior issues the students were struggling with at school. Lunches were catered in, and at the end of the day, the students rode the alternative site bus back to their home school and were sent home on their regular buses. The next day, the same process would take place. There would be new students each day, as well as those who had longer suspensions to serve.

The students were diverse in their cultural and ethnic backgrounds. Many were students of color, and most were from low-income families facing multiple issues. In many cases the parents were struggling with issues of poverty, unemployment or underemployment, or drug and alcohol problems; some were involved in criminal activities. Our staff were from ethnic and cultural backgrounds that matched those of the students, including staff who were bilingual.

This program had many twists and turns and was extremely labor intensive, both for school faculty and for the program staff. It demanded a great deal of time, and the challenge of coordinating with the school and transportation system was not easy.

One of the more interesting stories that resulted from this project was that many of the students did not want to return to their schools, but rather wanted to continue in the suspension program. They felt they were learning more with the individual help and felt safer in the alternative setting. They connected with the suspension staff, often adults who were from their same ethnic and cultural background. The students felt they were more respected and understood. Some of the time needed to be spent convincing the students not to reoffend so that they could return to the suspension site.

This program was well received by the schools that participated in the project. It seemed to be a no-brainer solution to help students succeed. Sending students who were already failing in their studies and causing disruption in the classroom to an unsupervised home for days on end was not a good solution. Unfortunately, like so many other common-sense approaches to dealing with difficult issues, programs end due to budget cuts or other hurdles too challenging to overcome.

This program and the others described in this chapter all could help children and adolescents who have been identified as struggling in their schools and homes. Sadly, many of these young people will also struggle as adults if they are not provided with the help they need to be successful and thrive.

Juvenile Day Reporting

Our staff developed the Juvenile Day Reporting (JDR) program to help youth who were battling with the negative forces in their lives. The county's juvenile probation division was challenged with increasingly high caseloads. The costs to place juvenile offenders in residential treatment facilities or correctional institutions were extremely high. To provide a better option for juveniles on probation, we developed a program to serve offenders in their communities, rather than in an institution.

The JDR program was housed in the same facility as our domestic abuse programs and had many unique features. It provided services Monday through Friday, after school until 8 PM. The participants either would find their own transportation or were driven by their probation officer or a JDR staff to the site. Once again, transportation required a major time commitment on the part of program staff or probation officers.

JDR served both male and female participants, ranging in age from thirteen to seventeen years. Their offenses included truancy, burglary, auto theft, drug possession, assaults, and other charges. Several of the participants had served time in a residential treatment or a juvenile correctional facility. Others were first-time offenders with lesser involvement in the juvenile justice system.

One of the main purposes of JDR was to provide at-risk juvenile offenders with adult supervision at one of the most critical times of the day. The hours from after school to eight o'clock at night were determined to be high crime periods when the juveniles were without adult supervision. We provided a setting in which the juveniles could be supervised and offered counseling to address their issues. In addition to criminal behavior, many were involved with gangs, alcohol and drugs, inappropriate sexual relationships, and school failures.

The participants all took part in meal preparation at the site. Each night they were responsible for cooking, serving, and cleanup. After the meal, they were assigned to a specific group to address different issues. These groups provided a therapeutic and educational approach to the various problems that were presented. A common issue was dealing with the participants' interactions with each other. Conflicts between the adolescents occurred frequently and were addressed in real time. Positive conflict resolution and communication skills were taught and practiced on a daily basis.

One of the most interesting experiences was the ride home in the van. The adolescents' conversations and behaviors were entertaining and at times challenging for the staff driver. Music requests and language were topics that always needed adult supervision until the last person was dropped off at their home.

This program, too, ended after several years due to funding cuts—and much to the displeasure of the probation officers who considered JDR a valuable alternative to incarceration. The program staff were talented and compassionate individuals whose dedication to these youth went unmatched. Their skills as therapists and mentors involved incredible patience and understanding of the complex lives these adolescents endured.

Women's Petty Theft Group

Our program offered a counseling group for women who were court-ordered for shoplifting offenses. The women were required to attend the group program as a condition of their probation.

Most of the women had money to purchase what they had stolen. Typically, they were middle class, were employed, and had stable living situations. A factor for some of these women was they had experienced a recent life-changing event, such as a death of a spouse or a divorce.

The group explored the different issues the women were experiencing and the relationship to their out-of-character shoplifting offenses. Some were suffering from depression and other mental health issues. Alcohol and drug use and abuse were addressed. The women also talked about abuse they had experienced in their relationships, but this subject was not the group's primary focus. Those who felt the abuse issue needed further attention were referred to the women's victims/survivors' groups.

Most of the women had never had any previous involvement with the courts. They felt very embarrassed and ashamed of their actions. The women found the group to be extremely valuable in providing them with the help and support they needed in their time of crisis.

Female Offender Program

A different group was designed to serve women charged with more serious crimes, such as forgery, child abuse/

neglect, prostitution, assault, and theft. This group of women had a very different profile from the women in the petty theft group. Some were seasoned offenders who had been involved in the criminal justice system for many years. A few were first-time offenders with no prior criminal records. Some women were hostile and resistant to the group. They would deny their behaviors and blame others and the system. In many instances, they displayed behaviors similar to those in the men's groups.

In addition to being involved in criminal activities, a common denominator for these women was that they were also victims of abuse. Most had been physically and sexually abused, either in childhood or as adolescents. Nearly all of these women reported abuse in their adult intimate relationships.

In these groups the counseling consisted of a blend of the treatment approaches used in the men's and victims/survivors' groups. Counselors addressed perpetrator behaviors as well as victim issues.

The majority of participants were cooperative and appreciative of the support from the group experience. They were held accountable for behaviors that brought them to the program, but also received support as victims. A few of the women later became involved in the women's victims/survivors' groups.

Women's Workhouse

In addition to providing the women offenders group at our facility, our staff conducted a similar group for women in a county workhouse. The women were charged with more serious offenses and were housed in a medium-security facility. A male staff member who also facilitated the men's groups led this women's group.

This was a challenging group of women, most of whom had long histories in the criminal justice system. Many had chemical and mental health issues that contributed to their criminal behaviors. Some had perpetrated abuse toward their intimate partners and their children. Some were engaged in prostitution, and most, if not all, had been victims of physical and sexual abuse.

The women voluntarily participated in the group, conducted once each week for ninety minutes at the correctional institution. Much of the curriculum that was used in the men's groups was applied in this group. The women's victims/survivors' groups curriculum was also useful to meet the women's needs.

The vast majority of the women in this program were perpetrators of abuse. Many were aggressive and hostile in their actions toward the other women in the facility, as well as toward the staff. The male therapist frequently had to address their inappropriate and aggressive responses, similar to managing the men's groups. However, the women's victim issues were also a critical need to be discussed. When I occasionally facilitated the group, I was also challenged by the women's attitudes and behaviors. The lives of these women were chaotic and full of abuse and neglect. Given their histories, much like those of the men we served, why would anyone expect them not to become perpetrators of abuse? They too were dealt a bad hand. The message remained the same for these women. There is no excuse for abuse, and it's up to each individual to make the change to end it.

Project Reconnect

A fourth program we offered to serve adult women on probation was called Project Reconnect. The women referred to this program by the court were assigned to a probation officer who would follow their case until it was closed. A female staff member from our program was also assigned to provide therapy and support for the women. In this experimental program, the probation officer would be assigned a limited caseload to provide highly concentrated services to the women.

These women were similar to the women in the workhouse program in that they had committed more serious crimes, many involving abuse and neglect of their children. Often a child protection worker was also involved. In many cases, the women had served jail or workhouse time and now were back in the community under close supervision.

This program provided an intense monitoring of the women's whereabouts, which included several unique factors. The assigned probation officer and the therapist were involved almost daily with the women. Their activities included making home visits; taking the women to doctor's appointments, job interviews, AA meetings, and grocery shopping; picking up children from school; and other daily life functions. All this effort was intended to help the women gain control of their lives.

This program was an experiment to see if this type of service would produce more favorable results for this population of women. It was hoped to be less expensive than incarceration and to be far more beneficial for the women and their families. The probation officers and our therapists provided several years of this service. It was challenging and exhausting work, with many successes as well as failures. The adult probation department viewed the program as a whole as highly successful. The program came to an end due to county budget cuts.

Strong and Peaceful Families

In 2006, the county's Joint Domestic Abuse Prosecution Unit and the Department of Public Health, along with our program, designed and implemented a service utilizing a multisystem approach to address the needs of adults and children who were impacted by family violence.

The services included case management, parent education, mental health counseling, transportation, access to daily activities, and interpreter assistance. This highly individualized approach served families who previously had lacked access to these resources. This partnership combined the courts, public health, and a therapeutic response to address the multiple issues these families faced.

Providing these comprehensive services to a select group of families was a one-of-a-kind approach to serving victims/survivors of domestic abuse. Our program's therapists who provided the hands-on services to the families were committed to the project's goals and worked tirelessly to meet the participants' many needs. Their dedication and competence were key to the successful collaboration and delivery of services. Sadly, like our other programs, it too came to an end due to monetary constraints.

African American Men's Group

After many years of conducting men's domestic abuse groups, we decided to offer a group specifically for African American men. These men had been ordered to our men's program and were given the option to attend a culturally specific group.

Our program was located in a predominantly black neighborhood, where many of the men lived or had friends and family. Some men would know each other or a family member. This connection could present an issue, especially if there was gang or drug involvement. For the most part, we resolved these issues and the group provided a positive counseling experience for its members.

At intake, we asked the men if they wanted to attend the African American group or the group for men of all ethnic backgrounds. The majority of the men chose the culturally specific group, although some were not interested in that option. African American male counselors who previously had facilitated the men's groups provided the counseling for the new group. The group was the same sixteen weeks in length, and all of the men were court-ordered to attend. In addition to following a similar men's curriculum, the African American counselors designed culturally sensitive exercises to acknowledge and support the men's specific needs.

We conducted a research study to compare the treatment results of the culturally specific/sensitive African American men's group to the non–culturally specific men's groups. The study's most noteworthy finding was a higher completion rate for African American men in the culturally specific/sensitive group than for African American men attending the non–culturally specific men's groups. This finding was significant in that even if the non–culturally specific men's groups were facilitated by African American counselors, the culturally specific men's group had a higher completion rate. Of course, the successful completion of any men's domestic abuse treatment group does not necessarily indicate that the abuse has stopped. The study did not follow the men after they completed the program.

Hmong Men's Group

Our city had one of the largest settlements for Hmong immigrants in the country. The Hmong were US allies in the

Vietnam War and lived primarily in the mountain regions of Laos. They provided intelligence for the CIA and fought against the North Vietnamese alongside American forces. The Hmong soldiers suffered tremendous losses, as did Hmong women, children, and elders. In the end, they were forced from their homes and country.

An increasing number of Hmong men in the community were being arrested for domestic assault. No programs offered a men's domestic abuse group in the Hmong language. The probation department asked if we could provide that needed service. A Hmong probation officer was assigned the caseload of Hmong men.

Several Hmong clinicians working in our program had undergraduate or graduate degrees in social work or psychology. One of our Hmong social workers who was bilingual in English and Hmong was interested in learning how to facilitate a group for the Hmong men. To our knowledge, this group would be the first of its kind to serve Hmong-speaking men in a domestic abuse group. For the next two years, I co-facilitated and trained two Hmong staff to lead the group. I was the only non-Hmong member in the group.

Most of the older men spoke only Hmong. While some of the younger men were bilingual, a number of the American-born members spoke very little Hmong. Many of these American-born men were uncomfortable with their Hmong language skills. At intake, the Hmong men who were bilingual were given a choice of a Hmong-speaking or English-speaking group. Several chose the latter, primarily because the younger Hmong men did not want to be identified with their elders. They did not share the same life experiences and did not always accept the cultural norms of their elders. The language barrier also played a role in their decision to choose the English-speaking group.

Co-facilitating the Hmong men's group was one of the

most interesting experiences of my career. The Hmong facilitators were exceptional young clinicians who were eager to learn the men's curriculum and how to facilitate a group.

The group members ranged in age from nineteen to fiftysomething. The majority of the older men had fought in the war and displayed visible wounds. Most were teenagers or in their early twenties when they fought in the war and were very proud of their military service. The younger men had been born in the United States and were very much Americanized.

The older men were unemployed, mainly due to the language barrier and because they did not have the skills or training to compete in the American workforce. They felt lost and inadequate in a country with customs and values that differed from their own. They would often speak of going back home to Laos. In the United States they were without a country and felt unwelcome. Like so many other immigrants, they were told to "Go back to where you belong." This attitude was devastating to the men who had fought and sacrificed so much to help the United States in the war. In their homeland they had status as clan leaders, farmers, or soldiers, and now they were without jobs, income, and homes to provide for their families. The inability to communicate in English left them adrift in a foreign land.

The Hmong men could not understand the American laws that did not allow them to abuse their wife or children. In their culture, the man was head of the family. Women did not have their own identity; their identity was with the man. Their role was to remain as a servant to the man and be silent about their needs. This tradition may seem to match some American men's thinking, but there were other cultural differences. Older Hmong men viewed having a second wife as acceptable and expected the first wife to approve of this arrangement. The clan, an important and significant force in the Hmong culture, primarily benefits the man. Hmong women are expected to stay in marriages, and divorced women are stigmatized. Other cultural barriers keep Hmong women in abusive relationships. In most instances in the Hmong culture, the man's actions would not be considered abuse. I was told there is no word in the Hmong language for "abuse."

The younger, American-born men knew the elders' thoughts and actions were not appropriate. They were familiar with the laws, and although they were raised in traditional Hmong families, they did not live by the cultural norms of the elder men. They knew that abuse was not acceptable in American society and were keenly aware of the cultural differences in how women were viewed. Oftentimes in group the younger members were embarrassed as they listened to the older members express their attitudes and beliefs. But it was difficult for the younger group members to challenge the older men on their thinking or behaviors. The Hmong culture holds a strong respect for elders. Even the younger Hmong counselors I trained found it difficult to confront the elders in the group. A cultural trait of the Hmong is to be respectful, polite, and soft-spoken. I had to work with the Hmong counselors to be more assertive in confronting the group and addressing the men's behaviors. There was a fine line of being disrespectful and holding the elders accountable.

Several Hmong clinicians, both male and female, became involved in working with victims/survivors as well as perpetrators of domestic abuse. Although it was challenging to address the clans and Hmong customs on this issue, great strides have been made to educate and support efforts to end abuse in the Hmong community.

Men's Jail Group

One final men's group was conducted in the county jail. This group was offered to the inmates on Saturday mornings. Sometimes being able to get out of their cells was reason enough for the men to attend. It was an open-ended group, which allowed in new inmates along with others who were already attending. Typically, a very small number of men participated, but those who did felt it was worth their time. Some returned every week, while others would come and go.

The curriculum was the same as in the men's domestic abuse groups, with a few added topics the men wanted to discuss. The inmates were made aware of the men's domestic abuse groups, and some were court-ordered to attend at a future date.

Domestic Abuse Training Program

In addition to providing counseling services to men, women, children, and adolescents, our program also offered workshops and trainings. These were done for a variety of groups, such as clinicians, police, child protection workers, clergy, college students, and faculty.

In-House Training

Following the training I presented for the Navy related to the couples counseling program (see page 124), other staff members and I conducted a series of trainings for military and civilian attendees. They spent a full week receiving program content and participating in all the group counseling sessions.

These clinicians were an amazing collection of individuals with diverse backgrounds and a variety of life experiences.

They were active-duty service members, government workers, civilian contractors, and retired military. They came from different commands and locations throughout the United States and abroad. Attendees from Canada and other local agencies wanted in-depth training on how to facilitate the various counseling groups we provided. We conducted a number of these weeklong trainings over the course of a couple of years.

The training participants commented that the hands-on experience of participating in the therapy groups provided them with the information needed to go back to their programs and conduct such groups with increased confidence. The men, women, and children who gave permission for the trainees to participate in their groups felt a sense of pride in knowing they were helping military families and others with this issue. Our staff, who conducted the training and facilitated the various groups, also felt good about providing this unique training experience. It was a lot of work and a big time commitment on everyone's part, but the long-term benefits made it worthwhile.

For several years, I was invited to conduct trainings at a variety of naval bases and ships throughout the United States and commands abroad. I talked with various groups, including commanding officers, officers and enlisted personnel, and civilian and government workers. I trained and worked closely with the Navy's Family Advocacy Program staff, who provided counseling services to the service members and their families. I also trained clinicians from the Army and other branches of service for their domestic abuse counseling programs.

It's been a number of years since my work with the military in their efforts to provide help to service members and their families on the issue of domestic abuse. I have lost track of their efforts and how they are dealing with this issue today. I had great respect and admiration for their commitment to providing the best treatment programs for their clients. As a veteran, I appreciate their choice to serve those who serve all of us. Our service members and their families deserve the best possible treatment and support to improve their lives. I was honored to be able to help clinicians who serve our military families address this critical issue.

No Guarantees

The programs described in this chapter were developed as additional resources to help men, women, and children. Some helped train hundreds of individuals working to end abuse. The programs serving children and adolescents were an attempt to intervene earlier in their lives to reduce the impact of the abuse. Yet, even four-year-olds already displayed emotional and physical signs that were troubling and heartbreaking. The counseling groups gave these children a positive outlet to safely talk about the abuse and receive the support of caring adults to let them know the abuse was not their fault. The middle-school students and the juveniles on probation needed guidance and supervision to help them change their aggressive and abusive responses toward others. They were given new ways to resolve their conflicts and talk about their problems and receive support for positive change.

Like the men's treatment groups, none of these services guaranteed that things would get better or the abuse in the participants' lives would end. However, the stories of adults and children who benefited from the counseling and support of these and other programs are well worth the time and money spent.

All Good Things Come to an End

The challenge that all businesses face in a world of limited resources is also present when confronting the issue of domestic violence. Our domestic abuse programs were funded through a variety of sources, including county corrections, grants, insurance, private fees, and nonprofit endowment funds. All of these funding sources were under constant pressure to reduce or eliminate spending, which often meant closures of programs and services.

The cold reality of funding cuts usually impacts populations most in need of services—the poor, disenfranchised minorities, children and adolescents, and other at-risk individuals in the community. The programs described in these chapters were all eliminated over time, not because they didn't fill a critical need and not because the problems were all solved, but because the monies were not available to continue to support the services. In the end, the critical needs of the individuals in these programs were left unresolved.

I trust our efforts were not in vain. Our programs provided thousands of individuals with the tools, resources, and support they need to live a violence-free life. Although our programs ended, many of the staff moved on to other settings where they continue to do the work. These remarkable people are still out there, spending their careers helping others, and they are asking for your help. It will take all of us to examine what role we can play in helping make our homes and communities a safe and violence-free place to live.

CHAPTER TWELVE

Conclusion

It's been a long journey for the reader to come this far in the book. I hope I have achieved my initial goal of providing a closer look at the issue of domestic abuse in our homes. Describing *The House* exercise and the inside workings of the men's and women's groups provides an experience usually witnessed only by therapists and advocates. This conclusion addresses a few final thoughts and answers questions generated in the previous sections.

Who Will Abuse?

Before I answer some of the critical questions about men's treatment groups, it is important to restate that not everyone who grew up in an abusive home will be abusive. In turn, there is no guarantee that someone who did not experience abuse in their childhood homes will not be abusive in their intimate relationships. Nearly all the men I served admitted that abuse was present or prevalent in their childhood homes. In the women's groups, some reported abuse in their childhood homes, but many did not. However, women also acknowledged that after attending the women's victims/survivors' groups, they were able to identify more abusive behaviors than they originally thought had occurred.

Jail or Treatment

In the early days of treatment programs for male perpetrators of domestic abuse the argument was that men who abused their partners should not get treatment. Domestic abuse was a crime and the offender must be punished. Allowing men to go to counseling instead of going to jail was giving them an easy way out. Battered women's advocates felt very strongly that perpetrators should be sentenced to jail.

It was hard to argue against the stance that men who were abusive deserved to be punished. Ordering jail or prison sentences would send a clear message that *domestic abuse is a crime*. The reality of the day was the courts were not ready to send domestic assault cases to jail. In most cases the courts would recommend probation with a suspended jail sentence. A condition of probation was the offender would complete a men's domestic abuse program. Failure to do so would result in a thirty- to ninety-day jail sentence.

Judges Meeting

I was invited to do a domestic abuse training for all the judges in the state. I had an hour to present *The House*, and I did the physical abuse room first. When I got to the verbal abuse room, the rumblings from the judges started. As I presented the emotional abuse room, the room got loud. The judges exclaimed that they could not sentence anyone who committed emotional abuse; there needed to be physical evidence.

They were probably right, but that wasn't the point. I wanted to show the judges that abuse comes in many forms and some of the most damaging abuse, such as emotional abuse, will never make it to their courtrooms. At that time, many judges still either were not sentencing domestic assault offenders or were giving light sentences. The hope was that the judges would see what else, besides physical abuse, goes on behind closed doors.

Fortunately, I had asked two men who had completed the men's program to join me for the presentation. One was an educated middle-class individual; the other was a younger man who had been involved in the criminal justice system for many years as a juvenile and adult offender. Each man told his story of how they were court-ordered to attend the program and their experience in it.

Their stories got the judges' attention. Both men reported that they initially believed they did not need to be sent to a counseling group. They denied they had a problem with abuse. They claimed they were wrongfully charged. Both men agreed that the counseling helped them and they never would have attended if it wasn't court-ordered. The younger offender made the biggest impression when he pointed out a couple of the judges in attendance. He was hoping to get the judge known as "the easy judge," who would likely go light on his sentencing. However, he got one of the other judges in the audience, who was known as "the tough judge." That judge ordered him into the program. Needless to say, it was an awkward moment for the "easy" judge in front of his peers. I never did finish building *The House*, but I didn't need to. The message was received.

The training opened the eyes of some of the attendees, providing them with an up-close and personal example of how they could use their position to address the problem. The importance of the bench to court-order treatment for the men was key. The men would not seek treatment unless they were ordered to do so. Ordering the men to treatment versus letting them off with a lesser sentence was critical. It was also crucial that if the man failed to complete the requirements of the treatment program, he would be sent to jail. The judges heard the two men say that the treatment did help, even though the men were dead set against attending. I could have brought a hundred men to that conference and most would agree with the two members who spoke. "I didn't want to go, and I wouldn't have gone if I wasn't court-ordered, but it did help."

Some of the judges met afterward with the two men and talked more about their treatment experiences. Several judges in the audience referred men to our program and were pioneers in changing their colleagues' views. Over the years I spent many hours in the courtroom talking with judges and victim advocates to make the changes needed to better serve both the victims and the perpetrators.

Length of Treatment

There has been a great deal of discussion regarding the "right" length of men's domestic abuse groups. Options ranged from a one-day workshop to a yearlong or longer treatment program. Our program consisted of a sixteen-week group treatment model. Sixteen was not a magic number; it was really just the beginning. One factor to consider when determining the length of the group was the "choice." The men referred to our program had the choice of going to treatment for sixteen weeks or jail for six months to a year. Some men chose jail over treatment. If the treatment were longer, more of the men would probably have chosen jail. Another factor was the cost. Initially, the county probation department funded most of the program, which was less expensive than housing men in jail. It was also understood that treatment was better than jail in the likelihood of stopping the abuse.

Research has been conducted to determine the most effective length of treatment for the men, but to my knowledge the verdict is still out. Most people agree that longer would seem to be the logical option. In chemical dependency recovery, a lifetime of counseling and support helps keeps people chemically free. The CD model of inpatient or outpatient treatment, followed by continuous support groups, has worked for decades, and has changed and saved people's lives. I believe treatment for individuals who have abused their intimate partners or children would benefit from a similar approach.

As I pointed out earlier, ending abuse in all its forms will take an incredible amount of work. It also must last a lifetime. Like the alcoholic or drug user, one can't just start and stop whenever one feels like it. There has to be a total and permanent end to the abuse.

My View

My recommendation is that men who are charged with domestic assault should be placed on probation and serve a jail sentence. The length of the sentence may vary, but jail time reinforces the message that *domestic assault is a crime*. At a bare minimum, it would get the man's attention. After the jail time is served the man would be required to complete a domestic abuse program. Ideally, the treatment approach would be comparable to the chemical dependency model.

Our program's strong relationship with county probation officers and judges was critical in holding men accountable. A specialized unit of probation officers assigned to domestic assault cases was formed and housed in our facility. This coordinated effort was key to monitoring the men's progress or failures throughout the time they spent in the program. If the man did not successfully complete the treatment program, the probation officer would revoke the man's probation and the judge executed his jail sentence.

Battered women advocates voiced concerns regarding the men's treatment program. They asked: "Who were the male counselors providing the men's treatment?" "Could these male counselors be trusted to hold men accountable for their abuse?" "Would they side or collude with the men?" "Could the counselors be abusers themselves?" These concerns needed to be addressed to establish trust between the women who served female victims/survivors of abuse and the male counselors who served the male perpetrators. The concerns were not easily resolved. The best way to build trust was to spend time with each other and ask the difficult questions. The staff and I spent countless hours working with victim advocates, court personnel, other program clinicians, and women's shelter staff, building collaborations to improve services to perpetrators and victims/survivors of domestic abuse. The Clinician's Corner appendix describes a controversial change we made to help address the question of facilitator accountability and credibility.

A Different View of the Abuser

Many people do not share the opinion that the men we serve deserve the help they are offered in a men's treatment program. In fact, most would have a hard time showing compassion or support of any kind, and understandably favor harsh punishment for their behaviors.

It might help us view these men differently if we think of them as young boys who lived in *The House*. Remember the story of the boy and his brothers, standing behind the bedroom door, wondering if their mother would be killed and if they would be next. So many boys either witnessed abuse or were the direct victims of abuse—probably both. If we had discovered them in their childhoods, we would have viewed them as victims. There would have been great concern and compassion for them. Hopefully, they would have been given all the support and help they needed.

It's a tragedy these men were never discovered as small boys or young men living in *The House*. They were victims and survivors of the abuse and neglect that formed their lives. They were "taught" abuse as an effective way to gain power and control over another person. These lessons set the stage for what was to come.

Fast-forward to them as adult male perpetrators of abuse. We do not view them through the same lens. I reminded the men to think about what damage the abuse in their childhood homes caused them, their siblings, and their mothers. It also destroyed their fathers. There are no winners when domestic abuse is present in the home. I also made clear that, as awful and sad as their situation was, it was time for them to face up to their own behaviors and stop the abuse in all its forms.

Unfortunately, the past cannot be changed. But we hope that having the men look at their own victimization will help them understand what their partners and children are experiencing. Our approach was not to rub their noses in it but rather to help them end the cycle of abuse and develop a sense of empathy and compassion for their victims. As children continue to be the victims/survivors of domestic abuse, we will continue to have adult perpetrators and victims.

What Is Considered Success?

A reduction in physical abuse means less injury and death. Obviously, this noteworthy outcome alone may be worth all the effort of treatment for men and could be claimed as a major success. But we know other forms of abuse have devastating and long-lasting effects on their victims. If the man's partner were abused only once a week, versus twice a week, how should this result be viewed? The reduction of any kind of abuse is a great accomplishment, but it is not the ultimate goal.

Men's domestic abuse programs, ours included, conduct research and offer anecdotal stories of men they serve. Some programs cite reduction in physical abuse to claim very high success rates in ending men's abuse. The problem with these claims is they only consider the decrease in one form of abuse. After building *The House* it should be clear that although reducing or ending physical abuse is an important accomplishment, there is often much more work to be done.

One last point regards some of the findings on recidivism rates. Research that claims treatment success based on the number of men who are re-arrested and charged with another act of domestic violence is problematic. Most, if not all, research shows a very small percentage of domestic violence incidents are actually reported to the police. This low rate is especially true in communities of color. Even fewer cases make it to court. Also, men are frequently very mobile and move from county to county or state to state. Criminal records do not always accurately track them. Many will find new victims.

There are men who have ended their abuse, and they need to be acknowledged. Programs serving male perpetrators of domestic violence have helped to reduce some men's abuse. Lives have literally been saved, yet it is difficult to determine the long-term impact of treatment for male perpetrators. In my experience, only a small number of men who completed treatment ended their abuse. Total elimination of *all* forms of abuse must be the ultimate goal.

What Other Options?

What else could be done to help men end their abuse? Imprisonment? In most instances incarceration isn't forever. Men will return to society to become intimate partners and fathers. There is no easy answer. In the men's treatment groups, some men did listen and admit to their abusive behaviors. Others remained stuck in their abusive ways of thinking and continued to abuse. Men who completed the program were given an opportunity to examine their lives and decide what future they would choose.

Keep in mind that the men our program served were court-mandated to attend treatment. Nearly 100 percent of the men attending the program were not coming to end their abuse. They were choosing the program as an alternative to jail. Still, roughly 75 percent of the men who started in a group finished the sixteen-week program.

There are men who voluntarily seek counseling for their abuse. Many are remorseful and have taken responsibility for their abusive behaviors. But these were not the men served in our program. It was extremely rare to have a man in one of our groups admit to his abuse and want help to change. If he successfully completed the program, he had a better chance of ending his abuse than most.

Who Will Change?

In the mid-'70s, I worked for six years as a counselor and group facilitator in a halfway house program for adult male felons. The men were eighteen to twenty-five years old, typically with long juvenile records. They were now in the adult court system facing three to ten years in prison for various felony offenses. They were offered an option to attend a residential treatment program in the community instead of serving their prison time. If they failed to complete the halfway house program, their prison sentences would be carried out. The program completion rate was about 50 percent, with an average stay of thirteen to sixteen months.

One man court-ordered to the halfway house was considered by most of the program staff as unlikely to succeed. He was hostile and resistant to any of the program rules. While other men in the program certainly shared these characteristics, his level of opposition was different.

Two important lessons from this experience remained with me my entire career. Not only did he successfully complete the program; he eventually became a volunteer in the program. He became a valuable asset in helping other men in the program turn their lives around. He was an example to his peers that change is possible. Lesson number one: nobody can ever be sure who will change and who will not. Lesson number two: because of me—and in spite of me—in my role as a counselor, a person could change.

Not surprisingly, several of the men from the halfway house program showed up fifteen years later in the men's domestic abuse groups on domestic assault charges. During their stay in the halfway house, the topic of domestic abuse was not explored or addressed. Hindsight tells me that many of these men were involved in abusive relationships. Violence in their childhoods was also not discussed.

Looking back, it is clear that issues of childhood abuse and domestic abuse both should have been a topic of their treatment. In that era, domestic violence was not something treatment staff were trained to address.

Based on my experience working with the population of men I served, only a very small number will end their abuse. It takes a great deal of work, and sadly, most men will not do the work. I didn't make any promises to the men except this one: "If you do the work it takes to end your abuse, it will be worth it. If you don't, the worst is yet to come."

Hope for Change

Reading the men's stories from *The House* may inspire a sense of dread or hopelessness. Successes were few and far between. Yet I still believe there is hope for some men to change. There is no magic wand to end abuse. It will only end with an honest commitment to change one's abusive behavior. This commitment requires a lifetime of work. I have witnessed and known men who have ended their abuse and improved their lives, and the lives of their children and partners. Dedicated women and men continue to provide support and counseling to victims/survivors and perpetrators of domestic abuse in the hope that their efforts will end the abuse and trauma that happens in *The House*. They are hopeful, and so am I.

Is It Worth It?

One might ask, "If the number of men who stop their abuse is so low, why would anyone bother to do all this work with these men?" Even if only one out of a hundred men ended their abuse, it would be worth it. One man ending his abuse impacts all those around him. His partner, children, grandchildren, and ex-partners—all would benefit. His changed behaviors could impact future generations and may end the generational cycle of abuse.

We shouldn't give up on anyone. I have seen some tough guys become vulnerable to accepting help. It was not a large number, but it did happen. The power of the group should never be underestimated. For many decades the group treatment experience has been successful in treating chemical dependency and other health and mental health issues. In the men's domestic abuse groups, it was powerful to watch a member you never thought would admit to having a problem break down and own up to his abuse.

I believe it is worth the effort to work with the men to confront their abusive behaviors and support change. Remember: you can lead a horse to water, but you can't make him drink. My goal was to make the men "thirsty" to change their lives for the better. A life without abuse was something most of the men have never known. My years of working with the men were challenging, and at times it felt like the mountain was too high to climb. Yet I felt compassion and hope for these men and believed the treatment experience, at a minimum, challenged their thinking. I know it helped many recognize the devastating impact abuse has had on their victims and on themselves.

The men who do end their abuse are the hope for the future. They have taken the steps needed to change. Their efforts will make a difference in their lives and the lives of others. I have witnessed these men take on the role of speaking out against their abusive behaviors, and I challenge others to do the same.

The bottom line is there is no excuse for abuse. A great deal of time was spent in every men's group holding the men totally responsible for their abuse. It was a constant struggle to confront them on their negative attitudes toward their partners or ex-partners. There was a fine line between listening to the men's concerns and, at the same time, challenging their faulty beliefs and accusations. I saw firsthand the lives of the men I served. It was not pretty. They lived lives most of us would agree were extremely damaging to everyone in their path, including themselves. Now they were in a position to make some major decisions for their lives and the lives of others. I spent over three decades trying to help such men examine their pasts and decide their futures. I never found the cure. My message was always that it would be up to each one of them alone to do the work to end their abuse. My ultimate hope is that someday *The House* will be a safe and violence-free place for all who live there.

End of the Program

After nearly three decades of providing critical services to women, men, adolescents, and children who suffered from the trauma created by domestic violence in their homes, our program was eliminated due to budget cuts. We were one of the largest, most comprehensive domestic abuse counseling programs in the country. We served thousands of adults and children and trained hundreds of clinicians and student interns. Our staff faced many challenges in helping men end their abuse. The work was hard, and the rewards often went unnoticed. All the programs required patience and understanding of the issues perpetrators and victims/survivors face in their lives. The staff, interns, advocates, and volunteers who provided these services were dedicated pioneers. They paved the way for future workers to continue to strive to end domestic abuse.

Sadly, our program, with its globally recognized and highly regarded treatment model, was abruptly ended. The problem of domestic violence didn't go away, but the decision makers in the organization chose to direct the monies elsewhere. The struggle to fund services for victims/survivors and perpetrators of domestic abuse persists. It should be clear by now that this issue will continue to have epidemic-like consequences for millions of families throughout this country.

Another Voice

A very good friend who read this book in draft form, and who has been a driving force behind my writing, challenged my conclusion. Given my account of the unfavorable results, he questioned whether it was really worth the money and effort to provide counseling for the men. Could the money be spent better elsewhere? He is not a coldhearted individual; in fact, for over thirty-five years he was a very successful family practice physician. In addition to working with his patients in the clinic and hospitals, he worked for years serving adolescents with severe drug and alcohol addictions. His questioning made me rethink a couple of issues.

First, the correctional systems designed to address domestic assault are not working. The majority of domestic assault cases are still prosecuted as a misdemeanor offense. Shoplifting and jaywalking are misdemeanor offenses. In some jurisdictions, domestic abuse cases still are not prosecuted. Or they are referred to the family court, not the criminal court. This initial step in domestic assault cases sends the wrong message to the offender. Many other assaults on strangers are charged as felonies. Recall my story about the pit bull ring: animal cruelty is often categorized as a felony. It is still rare that domestic assault cases are charged as felonies.

Doc and I agree that the consequences for the offenders need to be severe enough to address their behavior. If counseling is unsuccessful, longer jail or prison sentences, more supervision from the courts, and more directive and sustained probation need to be imposed. Treatment should be one component to the overall approach, but there should be more follow-up and long-term court intervention in domestic assault cases. The front end of the issue also needs to be addressed, everything from the appropriate police response to the prosecution, conviction, and sentencing of offenders.

Second, Child Protective Services is constantly placed at the mercy of misguided and ineffective laws that return children to unsafe homes. In many cases, the child is returned to the home where the abuse occurred. The perpetrator often is granted visitation rights or some form of custody because of their legal status as a parent. Parents who are abusive to their children should not be allowed to have contact with them. The children should be placed in a protective environment until there is evidence both that the parents are able to safely care for their children and that the abuse has ceased. In reality, the caseloads carried by probation officers and child protection workers are at an unmanageable number. In order to adequately provide the oversight needed to monitor and supervise the individuals involved, major staffing increases are needed.

The closure of programs like ours due to funding shortages doesn't make sense. Research as well as anecdotal stories of successful interventions document their positive impact. The argument to focus more monies on these types of programs seems logical.

Where will the monies to support efforts that will have a positive impact on the lives of children and adults come from? Adequate funding for agencies and institutions that serve the educational and mental health needs of children and adults has always been an uphill battle. All of the systems that support these types of services are stretched beyond their capacities. In order for real change to happen, a new agenda to meet the needs of those identified individuals and families must be put forth. Funding programs for children and adults earlier, when the issues arise, will prevent limited resources from being spent on costly and less effective alternatives.

Where Do We Invest?

I have often been asked, "Where should we invest our limited resources to have the most impact to end the abuse?" This essential question does not have an easy answer. I reply, "Focus on the children." However, then the question is, "How do we reach the children?" The men's stories of their childhood homes make it clear if we don't reach the children in *The House*, we will be catching them downstream as adults. For many, it's too late.

What Can We Do?

If we want to have fewer adult perpetrators and victims/survivors of domestic abuse, we need to reach the children. Regrettably, parents are not always in the best position to provide the support and help their children need. They may be dealing with their own issues or not have the capacity to intervene appropriately. Or the parent could be the perpetrator, and the children will continue to be the victims.

We need to find better ways to reach the children who are experiencing violence in their homes. This responsibility falls on all of us. It cannot be left to a county or state agency. Friends, neighbors, and relatives have the most contact with children living in these homes. Their actions or lack thereof could mean the difference. The next group of protectors includes teachers, clergy, coaches, police, medical professionals, and school counselors and nurses, as well as others who know these children and adolescents. Violence in *The House* should be everybody's concern.

People often feel that it is none of their business what others do inside their home. Many may not know how to respond. If you witnessed your neighbor's house being burglarized, wouldn't you call the police? You may even try to intervene. Why wouldn't someone confront or report a situation that involves children growing up in an abusive home? There is an option to report anonymously to the police or child protection. It's a phone call that can save a life or change a life.

Several years ago I heard what sounded like a domestic incident at a neighbor's house. I did not know the neighbor, but I knew there were children living in the home. You'd think I would have had no problem picking up the phone and dialing 9-1-1. After all, I should know exactly what to do. I did not immediately pick up the phone at 2 AM. I hesitated to get involved. But after a couple of minutes, I made the 9-1-1 call.

Role of the School

To reduce the number of perpetrators and victims, we need to address the problem on a number of fronts. One obvious example is the issue of bullying in the schools. Any teacher can tell you as early as preschool who the bullies are in their classrooms. The kids, especially their victims, know who they are too. It was disturbing to me as I worked with middle-school boys and girls the amount of bullying and unhealthy relationships that were happening. In many cases, these children are acting out troubles in their homes. The aggressive behaviors of these young bullies could be early indicators of future abuse issues down the road. While it is critically important to address the bullying behavior, it is also important to be aware of the possibility of violence in the home. These young perpetrators' behaviors need to be addressed by the adults in charge.

I can promise you that no matter what your age, you are able to name the bullies in your schools, from grade school on. We need to concentrate our efforts on helping both the bullies and the victims earlier in their lives. It shouldn't come as a surprise that several of the men in the men's groups were the bullies in their schools.

Teachers are overwhelmed with the number of behavioral issues they face every day in their classrooms. There must be more designated staff in the schools who have the time, training, and authority to address the acting-out behaviors of the students. With adequate resources (mental health professionals), schools are where many problems can be revealed and could be addressed early enough to make a difference.

Teachers often comment that their job is to teach, not to be disciplinarians or therapists. And teachers can be some of the most influential individuals in children's lives. Their influence can be positive or negative, but the fact is they often spend more time with the children than do the parents. They have unique relationships that can help shape the minds and actions of the children in their classroom. Sending clear messages to students about how to treat others and what is acceptable and unacceptable behavior is something that teachers can do. And they have the opportunity to notice behaviors that can signal abuse at home. Outstanding teachers take these actions with great skill and commitment.

We need to find new ways to reach our children and adolescents who are the perpetrators and victims of violence. Whether it be in the home or at school, the issue must be addressed. It starts by openly talking about it and giving permission for children and adolescents to seek help and support from adults. Curriculums that address healthy relationships should be required. Some schools are doing work in this area.

Coaches for school sports teams can also play a critical role in providing clear messages to their athletes about what behaviors are not acceptable on or off the field. The attitudes and behaviors of young males toward females are often on display in locker rooms as well as in classrooms. Consistent messages from teachers and coaches alike can help direct these unacceptable views early on. Chapter 11 describes several programs we developed to address some of these issues.

Mentors

Think for a moment: Who in your life has had a positive impact on you? If you're lucky, you may be able to list several people. It may have been a parent or even both parents. It may have been a neighbor, a teacher, a coach, or an older sibling. Research shows that a child needs only one such positive person to make a difference in their life. Acting as a positive mentor/role model is one of the most important gifts any one of us has to offer (Search Institute, Developmental Assets Framework, 2011).

When I think about the people who had a positive impact on me, the first one who comes to mind is my mother. Another is my paternal grandmother. One unusual influence was my next-door neighbor, Earl. He was a tall, gray-haired man whose false teeth were brown from chewing tobacco. He suffered from severe epilepsy. He was unable to work, so when all the neighborhood fathers were gone every day, he was home working in his yard and garden. He was married with no children. He always had dogs.

Earl was known by every kid in the neighborhood. In today's world, parents might consider him odd or possibly even a threat to their child. There was never any inappropriate behavior; he was just an old man who loved to tell us stories, most of them untrue. His days were spent playing baseball in the streets with all of us kids or joining in snowball fights. Earl raised the kids in our neighborhood. He was a man with no education, no children of his own, no wealth or material possessions, yet he was the father most of us never had. He was there for us every day and played the games we loved to play. I never thought of him as a mentor; he was just Earl. But that's all the neighborhood kids needed: someone to play with and tell us stories and show us that we were important and belonged.

My list also includes an eighth-grade teacher and a football coach who had a positive influence on who I am today. A Navy chief petty officer, a supportive supervisor, a college professor, and a list of others played significant roles in my life. I am one of the fortunate ones who had many mentors.

Anyone can be a mentor and make a difference in a child's life. Volunteering at schools, community and church programs, and Big Brothers Big Sisters are just some ways to become a mentor.

When I was in the eighth grade, I coached a neighborhood baseball team of fourth graders. I was the "older brother" or Earl these boys looked up to. Many years later, I kept in contact with a few of these now grown men. They had successful business careers, and one became a doctor. I didn't view myself as a mentor. I didn't have any money or special talent; I just had time. Time is one of our most valuable resources, and if we share it with someone, it can change their life.

One day I was sitting in a college classroom when two people came to ask for volunteers to help tutor some junior high kids with their studies. One thing I learned in the military was never to volunteer. But in this case I did, and I was assigned to a seventh-grade boy who was on juvenile probation and living in a foster home. He was struggling with his schoolwork and was also having behavior problems at school. We spent the school year together working on his assignments, but mostly just talking about his days and his life at the foster home. We would go to McDonald's and play some games and just hang out. The next thing I knew, several other boys were asking if I would help them too.

That experience as a twenty-two-year-old probably had more impact on me than I had on those boys. I realized the power positive relationships could make in someone's life. It certainly made a difference in my life. We all have that power; we just need to share it. Today, I have neighbors and friends who are in their seventies and eighties and read to elementary kids in their schools. Another acquaintance volunteers at a battered women's shelter, and still another is teaching kids how to play the guitar. It is never too late to be a mentor. Try it: you will like it.

We also know, as we have read in these pages, that one person can have a negative impact. Sadly, this was the case for so many of the men, women, and children involved in the domestic abuse groups. Again, I think about all the stories I heard from the men about their childhood and adolescence. What a difference it could have made if a positive mentor had entered their young lives and let them know they were important to someone. Mother Teresa said that being "unwanted, unloved, or uncared for" was the worst thing possible for any human being to experience. She described the life experiences of most, if not all, of the participants in the treatment groups.

We can't wait for our systems to serve those in need of support. As a friend, a neighbor, a church member, a brother or sister, you might be the one to make the difference in someone's life. We can all look for the warning signs that someone could be a victim of abuse. We can ask questions and seek resources to help support those who are experiencing abuse in their lives.

An Epiphany

My original intent for developing *The House* was to come up with a way to help men in the domestic abuse groups recognize their abusive behaviors. While writing this book an epiphany happened: I realized that *The House* exercise was not only for the men in the groups, but that its greater purpose could be to help *all of us* increase our understanding of what constitutes abuse in intimate relationships.

I gave examples throughout the book where this exercise was presented in multiple settings. In all cases, it generated a discussion and response from the audiences. People's eyes were opened and their awareness was increased. I had forgotten that not only was *The House* building exercise valuable in helping perpetrators and victims/survivors recognize the abuse, but it also had a significant impact on all who participated in its presentation.

For many years, I was asked to conduct *The House* exercise at various colleges. It was one of my favorite experiences. In social work classes, women were the majority and were eager listeners. The male students always looked a bit uncomfortable but were able to engage in the process. The same held true in presenting the exercise with law students. Many of the female students revealed they had friends who they believed were in abusive relationships and this exercise helped solidify their concerns. Several students began to examine their own intimate relationships. The men also commented that the presentation made them think differently about the topic.

This exercise can be conducted by anyone in any number of settings. It doesn't take a social worker or psychologist to present it. Teachers, youth workers, clergy, chemical dependency counselors, shelter staff, medical personnel, victim advocates, PTA participants, and anyone who has an opportunity to talk with people can conduct this exercise. I presented *The House* to middle school and high school students with little modification, and they were fully engaged.

Hopefully, *The House* exercise will provide the reader with a framework to better understand the issues perpetrators and victims/survivors face in their lives. Their stories are disheartening and tragic. Our communities and our country will need to decide if violence in our homes will become a priority or if it will remain "a secret." Our jails and prisons are full of men and women who grew up in *The House* described in this book. Mental health clinics are overwhelmed with adults and children who suffer from trauma caused by abuse in the home. In chapter 1, I identified readers I hoped would find value in reading this book. Each of us can play a vital role in helping someone who is experiencing abuse in their lives.

I hope readers of this book will think about the audiences they might be able to reach. While *The House* may not be a topic at your next dinner party, your understanding of the concept raises the question: "What role can I play in addressing domestic violence in my community?"

The Clinician's Corner

This addendum explores several subjects, including female and male group facilitators, co-facilitation of groups, student interns, self-disclosure, types of groups, and rules violations.

The Facilitators

Who takes charge of the groups is a critical factor. The men's and women's groups were led by either one or two facilitators. One of the most powerful lessons we learned was who should facilitate men's and women's groups. At the start of our program only my female colleague and I facilitated the groups. She facilitated all of the women's victims/survivors' groups, and I led all of the men's groups.

This approach went on for several years, but as the program grew larger, we hired more staff. We continued the practice that the male counselors facilitated men's groups and the female counselors facilitated women's groups.

A Facilitator Exchange

At a certain point in the group, usually near the end of the program, the women's counselor was invited to address the men's questions and give them a woman's perspective about the abuse. The same held true for the male staff, who joined the women's group for a question-and-answer session. The men's and women's counselors remained in their respective group with the guest facilitator.

These facilitator exchanges produced some animated discussions. Not all of them were positive, especially in the men's groups. The men frequently became defensive and even aggressive toward the female counselor. The male facilitator would often have to intervene and redirect the men's questioning and hold the men accountable for their inappropriate behaviors.

The counselor exchange experience in the women's groups was entirely different. The male facilitator was welcomed, and the women were genuinely interested in hearing what the male counselor had to say. Their questions were respectful and appropriate. The counselor exchange was a very powerful experience for both the women and the men facilitators.

A Change Is Coming

It wasn't long after those early counselor exchange experiences that the female counseling staff began questioning what was happening in the men's groups. The conversations became personal, and tension developed between the male and female staff. The male counselors leading the men's groups felt like the female staff were questioning their ability to effectively address the men's abuse. Given the behaviors of the men's group members toward the female guest speakers, it was hard to argue otherwise. The male staff were not defending the group members' behaviors; they were embarrassed and concerned about the lack of progress the men had made in their treatment.

Male/Female Facilitators

We made the major decision to have male and female counselors from the women's and the men's groups co-facilitate in both groups. No other program that we were aware of at that time had done this. This change, especially having a male in a women's victims/survivors' group, was scrutinized by some other programs.

In terms of how this new combination of male and female group facilitators would work, many issues came into play. The first matter was how the facilitators would work together in the newly assigned groups. No female staff member had facilitated a men's group and vice versa. Some of the female staff did not want to co-facilitate a men's group and felt intimidated by and fearful of that experience. In addition, they worried that the male co-facilitator might dominate or control the men's group, setting up the female facilitator as "lesser than" or incapable of facilitating the group.

Because none of the male counselors had facilitated a women's group, several serious questions came to the fore: "How would women who have been abused by their male partners feel about having a man in their group?" "Can women talk openly about their most intimate issues with a male in the group?" These and other dynamics needed to be addressed in both groups.

After we initiated this facilitation change, we never went back to our previous practices. During many years of co-facilitating groups in this manner, we continued to address various complications as they developed. Given some of the differences in facilitating styles, the setup didn't always work, but overall it was one of the best decisions we made as a program.

Co-Leadership

For most of my early years facilitating men's groups, I was the sole facilitator in the group. Having two facilitators in the group brings advantages and disadvantages, regardless of whether the group is male/female co-led, male/male co-led, or female/female co-led. For all the groups we provided, there were many factors to consider when co-leadership was involved.

Each facilitator has a particular approach. Different styles, skill sets, and experiences can either make or break a co-facilitator combination. There are many examples of what can go right and what can go wrong with co-facilitating a group, and over the years our staff experienced the best and the worst.

One of the biggest factors that determined the outcome of the co-facilitation experience was the level of trust between the two facilitators. Their relationship proved vital to the group. You can probably imagine what could happen if the two leaders were on different pages from each other.

Building Co-Leadership

An early hurdle was that new female staff and female interns had never facilitated a men's group. Regardless of preparation beforehand, it was always a challenge for first-time co-facilitators to find their voice or role in the group.

A female co-facilitator who was co-leading her first men's group had to learn to take an equal facilitating role. Initially, the experienced, male facilitator took a more dominant role in leading the group. Later, we addressed this less-than-ideal setup. Individuals who had previous experience in other treatment groups were able to play a more significant role from the start.

It was important that time prior to every group session was spent clarifying what each facilitator's role would be in that group session. It could be as simple as who will start the session or who will lead an assigned topic or exercise. It was equally important to spend time after each group session discussing how the co-leadership was working. The co-leaders' preparation and debriefing was a critical factor in building trusting relationships.

Female Co-Facilitators in Men's Groups

In a men's group, the female facilitator might confront the men on their sexist or abusive language toward women. Often the men would look to the male facilitator for his response. It was important that he support his co-leader without seeming to come to her rescue. The male facilitator's response could contribute to the men's thinking that the female co-leader was the weaker party or she was one of those "flaming feminists." In addition, it would not be exclusively the female facilitator's role to confront men on their sexist attitudes or comments. The male co-leader needed to share equally in calling men out on their chauvinist and damaging way of thinking.

The female co-leader's voice of "equal power" needed to be established early on in the men's group. It's difficult to explain all the dynamics that occurred between co-facilitators of the groups. But when equal and consistent co-leadership was successfully in place, it was the most effective method of group treatment. We learned that male/female co-leaders was the best combination to provide treatment groups for men who abuse. Out of necessity, we continued to have men's groups led with only male staff. We also had men's groups that were co-facilitated by two female therapists. This combination was not ideal. Several of the female therapists described the toll it took on them to constantly confront men's attitudes and beliefs about women. Never did a male therapist lead women's victims/survivors' groups without a female therapist.

Male Co-Facilitators in Women's Groups

As we shifted to the co-facilitator model, our experience with the women's groups was much the same as with the men's groups. No male counselors had ever co-facilitated a women's victims/survivors' group. Again, most of the interns as well as new staff had never had these experiences.

The important difference for male co-facilitators in women's groups was that the male's co-facilitator role in the group was clearly secondary. The goal was not like that of the men's group, where the female co-facilitator was to be equal to her male counterpart. The secondary role of the male co-leader remained that way throughout the group. The imbalance of power the women had in their abusive relationships should not be present in their group experience.

I was able to spend hundreds of hours in the women's groups—one of the most significant and informative experiences of my career. The women were hesitant to have a male in their group, and rightfully so. Their level of trust for men was extremely low. The fear of talking openly about their situations in the presence of a male could be very uncomfortable and deeply concerning. Could he be trusted and would he be empathetic to the abuse experiences the women had endured?

In the end, response to the male/female co-facilitated

women's groups was overwhelmingly positive. The women's responses reaffirmed that this experiment of female/male co-facilitation had more ups than downs. The women felt strongly at the end of their experience that having a positive, "healthy" male in the group provided them with some hope that not all men were abusers.

I spent thousands of hours facilitating men's groups and felt competent in that work. However, being in the women's groups provided me with a far better understanding of the issues victims/survivors faced than if my experience had only been with the men.

The men would often ask, "What happens in those women's groups?" They strongly believed the women were being brainwashed with anti-male propaganda. One thing became very clear to me as a co-leader in the women's groups. I brought this revelation back to the men, telling them, "I watched women take giant steps forward in figuring out what they need. Unfortunately, many of you have taken only baby steps or one step forward and two steps back, and in some case, no steps at all."

Co-Leadership Gone Wrong

Not all co-facilitator pairings were successful. In fact, some were disastrous. These bad pairings happened with two male co-facilitators and also with male/female co-facilitators leading men's groups. It's telling that I did not hear of any bad experiences when there were two female co-facilitators leading men's groups. There were far fewer of these pairings, but it is still a revealing fact. One can imagine the damage that could occur in either a men's or a women's group if the co-facilitators were at odds with each other. Although rare, when these scenarios did occur they were immediately addressed.

A Story That Tells It All

I facilitated an aftercare group for men who had completed the sixteen-week program. The group was voluntary, and the numbers varied between five and ten men in the group. New men entered the group at different points and introduced themselves to the other members.

I'll never forget when a new member joined our group and happened to mention that Linda was his group leader. All of the other men had had male group leaders. They were totally puzzled by what the new member said. They asked him again: "Who facilitated your group?" He told them it was Linda. The other men said they couldn't imagine having a female facilitator. The new member responded that he couldn't imagine otherwise.

Several men's groups were facilitated by female therapists. The men's reactions to a female leader varied, especially at the beginning of the group. The overall response of the men was overwhelmingly positive; however, the setup did not go without challenges. The men's inappropriate behaviors and lack of boundaries frequently surfaced. For example, men would ask the female therapist out on a date or ask her personal questions about her dating relationships or marital status. The female leaders had to confront these advances and comments. Far fewer of those issues arose when male therapists were facilitating the groups. The topic of "self-disclosure" in group treatment is explored later in this addendum.

Today it is common practice to have male and female facilitators in men's treatment groups for domestic abuse. Less often there are male co-facilitators in victims/survivors' groups, but in our experience, when done correctly, this approach was viewed favorably by the women participants.

Student Interns

During our three decades of providing counseling services, hundreds of undergraduate and graduate students were assigned to perform their internships at our program. The vast majority had never facilitated groups, much less groups serving perpetrators and victims/survivors of domestic violence. There were far more female students than male students. Social work, marriage and family, psychology, and chemical dependency programs were the primary disciplines.

The students co-facilitated all of the various groups we offered. The women's, men's, children's, and adolescent groups were all part of their learning experience. Some were also involved in the other programs described in chapter 11. Some students were apprehensive of working with a particular population, such as the men's groups. Almost without exception, the interns felt they learned things they never would have experienced if they hadn't been encouraged to stretch their thinking. At a minimum, some learned what they didn't want to do in their future careers.

Self-Disclosure

Opinions regarding the use of self-disclosure by therapists with their clients are numerous. In the chemical dependency (CD) field, self-disclosure is a common practice where the vast majority of counselors use it effectively when working with individuals in treatment and recovery. In fact, at Alcoholics Anonymous meetings, the introduction is "Hello, my name is John and I'm an alcoholic."

Self-disclosure is an important topic that staff and student interns should discuss.

There is a place for self-disclosure; however, it needs to be strategic in nature, with a clear purpose. Used on a limited basis, it can have a powerful impact on the individual or group. I rarely used self-disclosure as an intervention in the men's groups. When I did use it as an intervention strategy, the message was well timed and carefully calculated.

In my years of facilitating groups at the halfway house with the men convicted of felonies, a common question was: "Have you ever committed a felony?" What they were really asking was whether I had anything in common with them or if I had walked in their shoes. They would also ask if I ever used drugs or alcohol. The list of personal questions would go on. They wanted to know if I could relate to them and if I had any credibility in understanding their problems. In CD treatment and recovery, many counselors are recovering from alcohol or chemical abuse. Self-disclosure gives them credibility and provides hope to individuals trying to get sober. I wasn't going to go out and commit a felony or become an alcoholic or abuse my partner so I could relate to the men. I needed to prove that I would listen to them non-judgmentally and hopefully gain their trust. I was there to help them with their problems and to support them in their efforts to live better lives.

Deciding what, if any, personal questions asked by clients should or shouldn't be answered is a difficult challenge. I addressed this topic with new clinicians and student interns prior to them going into a men's group. I prepared them for what questions they would be asked and how best to respond. It was an important skill to teach those who had not been asked questions such as: "Have you ever been abusive?" "Are you married?" "Do you have kids?" "Do you spank your kids?" "What would you do if you caught your partner in bed with someone else?" "Do you drink?" "Are you gay?" "Do you really believe this shit you're telling us?"

I advised the clinicians and interns to think about the purpose or outcome they are trying to accomplish when making the decision to self-disclose. There are times where doing so would be appropriate and beneficial to the therapeutic relationship. At other times, self-disclosure can have an unintended ill effect.

Types of Groups

The most common types of counseling groups are described as closed-ended or open-ended groups. Closed-ended groups start with the participants on the same date and end on a given date. No new members are added after the group starts. The open-ended group allows new members to enter the group at different points in time.

There are advantages and disadvantages to both types of groups. The most significant benefit of a closed-ended group was that the men were able to start and finish together as a group. The bonds between them became apparent, and they were able to witness the change in each other's aptitudes and progress, or lack thereof. They knew each other's stories and had taken risks and talked about things they had never imagined discussing. The men experienced an unspoken celebration at the end of the group, knowing they had successfully completed it while others had not. Often the men would exchange phone numbers and claimed they would stay in contact.

In the open-ended group, some men would be completing the group, while others were just starting. There was less of a bonding experience among the men because of this coming and going of group members. The advantage to this type of group was new arrivals were far less vocal regarding their anger at being there. For the most part, they were less challenging while they figured out the lay of the land. Ideally, the men who had been in the group for a period of time were able to show positive leadership toward the new members.

Both of these types of groups provide a treatment approach that can work. I enjoyed observing the different group dynamics these two groups displayed.

Group Size

The size of the men's groups varied. Usually there would be from ten to sixteen men in the group. An ideal group size is eight to ten members. Starting with a larger number was important. Given the high attrition rate in court-ordered groups, a smaller group at the start means it's possible to end up with only three to five men. This number is too small for a good group experience.

Group Length

The men's groups met for two hours, one time per week for sixteen weeks. The original length of the meeting was two and a half hours, with a ten-minute break. The breaks allowed for some interesting conversations among the men and some outside-of-group bonding, not all of which was positive. There was time for a bathroom break, a smoke, or a phone call, but it was always a challenge to get the men back into the group and refocused. Thus, a two-hour, no-break session worked far better for the men's short attention spans and incurred less disruption of the group process.

Group Rules

Originally, the men were not allowed to miss any of the sixteen sessions. The only excuse for missing a group was that they were in the hospital or dead. It was an uphill battle and an unrealistic expectation for the men to succeed in attending all of the sessions without a miss. Too much valuable group time was wasted dealing with men missing groups. We learned this lesson and changed our approach.

The new rule was clearly stated at intake and repeated in the first group session. A person could miss two groups in an eighteen-week period of time. In other words, if the man had perfect attendance, he would complete the group at week sixteen. If the man missed one session, he would finish in week seventeen. If he missed two sessions, he would finish in week eighteen. Three misses were grounds to be terminated from the program.

This rule dramatically reduced the time spent in the group discussing attendance. I strongly encouraged men to use their misses wisely. If they took misses early in the group process, I warned them they would be jeopardizing their chances of finishing the group.

Everyone needed to attend the first session or they would not be allowed to start the group. We would make a rare exception, but the first group session was critical in terms of laying out rules and expectations.

Late for Group

It was essential for the men to be on time for the start of group. The agreement was the group would start on time and end on time. If a member was late, the door would be closed and he would not be allowed to attend the group session. It would count as a missed group. The men would test this rule. It was important to enforce it or the group would continue to be disrupted by late arrivals.

Group Decisions

Even with explicit rules, exceptions needed to be considered, especially when it came to attendance and lateness issues.

Depending on the situation, I let the group members decide what the verdict should be. For example, if a man was late or missed his third group and he was halfway or more through the program, I would let the group decide whether or not to let the member continue. Of course, if the facilitator is not going to go along with the group's decision, this option should not be offered. But in the right scenario, it's beneficial to include the group in the decision-making process.

Usually, the group would decide to give the man one more chance, but with a stern warning or set of conditions. This group option had far more of an impact than if the facilitator alone made the decision. Sometimes the group members did tell the man he had his chances, and they would vote him out of the group.

Group Rule on Chemical Use

The rule regarding alcohol or drugs required the men to be sober and drug free on the day of group. If a person was suspected of being under the influence, he would be asked to leave the group and it would be counted as a missed group. Depending on the conditions of his probation, it could also mean immediate termination from the program.

Given the majority of the men's histories with drugs and alcohol, this rule was always going to be an issue. Sometimes it was obvious when someone was high or drunk, but many times the facilitator or group members couldn't tell. Or if the group members were aware that another member was high, they weren't going to bust him out.

It was critical for the counselor to make clear that this was everyone's group, and it was disrespectful and a waste of everybody's time if someone came to group under the influence of drugs or alcohol. It wasn't only the counselor's job to determine who was high; it was everyone's responsibility.

If a man in the group was asked to leave the session because of being under the influence, he would be given the opportunity to contact his probation officer the next day and tell of his violation. We made a follow-up call to the probation officer as well.

Many things needed to be considered when deciding whether to remove a man from the group. A close working relationship between the counseling staff and the probation officer was a critical factor when making decisions about the man's future in the program.

Confidentiality, Exceptions to the Rule

Group members needed to know that several items could not be kept confidential. Chapter 4, on setting the group rules and expectations, covers some of this information. The statement "what's said in group stays in group" has a few exceptions. The obvious ones include reporting to the probation officer any missed group meetings or any disclosed incidents of abuse.

Another exception is the "mandated reporting law" that requires clinicians and other professionals to report to authorities certain incidents of threats of violence, neglect, or abuse. Counselors facilitating the treatment groups were required to report any issues of child abuse or neglect. Also, the "duty to warn" reporting law applied if the counselor felt a person posed a threat to harm someone else or himself. In those cases, the proper authorities needed to be notified.

Another strict confidentiality violation would be if men talked about what other men said in the group with others outside of the group. The men could talk with others about what they themselves said in the group, but not what the other members reported. This violation of confidentiality would be grounds for removal from the group.

Wrap-Up

The topics covered in this chapter pertain to many counseling and support settings and are among the major ones we encountered in the types of services our programs provided. Of course, many other issues related to providing these services are not mentioned here. Hopefully, my experiences and those of our staff will aid others in their work.

APPENDIX 2

Military Treatment Challenges

My experiences working with the military and with clinicians who provide domestic abuse treatment for service members prompts me to briefly describe some of the differences between the military and civilian worlds.

Many complex scenarios that exist in the military and are not present in the civilian community can impact the response to domestic violence. One significant difference is that the men in the military have jobs that require them to be mobile. Frequent deployments and trainings are essential for military readiness. When a sailor or marine is mandated to a treatment program, this requirement becomes a problem for his command. Ships and shore assignments need the service members to perform critical tasks. The same can hold true with other branches of service when troops need to be mobilized.

The military's leverage over the service member is significant. The member's job or career could be on the line. In the civilian world, the employer more than likely would never know about the man's abuse or court involvement.

Another significant difference between the two systems is that men in the civilian community who are charged with domestic assault can go virtually unnoticed by friends or colleagues. In the military setting the service member's privacy regarding his situation is difficult to maintain.

While I was consulting with program development in the military, the command views on service members assigned to domestic abuse counseling ranged from terminating the member from service to fully supporting the treatment requirements. The responses and attitudes from the men's commands were understandable. It was a complicated issue with no easy solution. Meeting the needs of the military versus meeting the needs of the service member and his family created a major dilemma for both sides. Often these two sets of needs could not be met simultaneously.

Men and women enter the military for many reasons. For years there was the draft; today it's a volunteer service. Some may join for the training and job opportunities or educational benefits the military provides. Others might view it as a patriotic duty or a family tradition. Many benefits come with military service. And, of course, there are the downsides of family separations and wars.

Another reason for enlisting is the person may see the military as an escape from a violent home or abusive relationship. Typically, the new enlistees are young men and women in their late teens or early twenties. The military might be viewed as a place to provide safety and shelter for someone who is being or has been abused. This reasoning can be especially true for young women entering the military.

An enlisted member's military experience is very different from that of an officer. It is not glamorous, and many times it is not rewarding, especially in the early years of serving in the lower ranks of the military hierarchy. The everyday stress on a young adult away from home, friends, and family can be dramatic. The maturity levels of most eighteen- or nineteen-year-olds, even in the civilian world, are still in development. Add the military experience, a new marriage, and a long-term deployment, and things may not look like what the recruiter portrayed. The stress of all these new life situations can be overwhelming. Add a combat experience to this scenario, and there may be even more serious challenges the service member and his family will face. Domestic abuse, chemical abuse, depression, post-traumatic stress, and other mental health issues plague many of our military families today.

The life of an officer in the military has its own level of stress and challenges. Officers and enlisted service members share some of the same issues, like deployments and other stressors. The majority of officers are older and have college and other life experiences that most of the young enlistees lack. At the time I was working with the Navy and Marines, the issue of domestic abuse in the officer ranks was not getting the same attention as it was in the enlisted population. I don't recall officers being served in the groups with the enlisted personnel. There were senior enlistees in some of the groups, but not officers. To mix officers with enlisted service members creates a complex dynamic that does not exist in a men's counseling group in the civilian world. Even having senior enlistees mixed in with lower enlisted members can be problematic. The military's hierarchal structure creates a difficult issue related to treatment for its members. Providing counseling for the various ranks of the military in one setting is complicated and probably futile. The military hierarchy is too entrenched and could cause unfavorable outcomes for all parties involved.

Rank or status does not prevent someone from being

abusive. The commands struggled with all members who were charged with domestic assault. Confronting officers or senior enlisted members presented even more challenges due to their career status and specialized training that was critical to the mission.

ACKNOWLEDGMENTS & THANKS

I would like to name all of the people who have shared so much of their lives doing this work. But if I named one, I would risk leaving someone out. Instead, I will thank them more generally, and hopefully all will know who they are.

First, I would like to thank the thousands of women, men, children, and adolescents who were participants in our programs. Some came reluctantly, but they shared their stories of the horrors of violence in their homes. They are the ones I remember the most.

The hundreds of staff members and interns I had the privilege to work with over the past three decades are the unsung heroes. They worked day in and day out, in the trenches, listening to and helping those who were in dire straits. Often, they were dealing with life-or-death situations. Only a finite number of individuals have the strength and desire to do the work they do.

I also want to thank all of the other workers from the women's shelters, the victim advocates and intervention programs, the courts, probation, the police, judges, the schools, medical staff, and others who spent their careers helping those who are at risk.

A special thanks to Gayle, Doc, Ruth, Rob, Jody, and Yvonne, who helped me get my thoughts down on paper. Without them, this book would still be in my head, never to see the light of day.

Great appreciation and recognition goes to Shannon Pennefeather and Peter Tepp, whose exceptional work helped me shape my experiences and words, as well as to Judy Gilats, whose design skills brought my stories to book form.

Last, but not least, I want to remember four women who were gone too soon: Kay-Laurel, Shelia, Sharon, and Ellen.

My hope is that our society will continue to address the impact violence in the home has on its victims. I also hope that programs serving the men who have been abusive to their intimate partners and children will not give up on their efforts to help the men end their abuse.

My ultimate hope is that someday *The House* will be a safe and violence-free place for all of us who live there.

RESOURCES

National Domestic Violence Hotline:
1-800-799-7233 (SAFE)

Centers for Disease Control and Prevention: cdc.gov

National Coalition Against Domestic Violence: www.ncadv
.org

Olweus Bullying Prevention Program: https://olweus.sites
.clemson.edu/

Planned Parenthood of the Southwest Ohio Region,
checklist for recognizing unhealthy relationships:
https://www.plannedparenthood.org/planned-parent
hood-southwest-ohio

Search Institute, Developmental Assets Framework, 2011:
https://www.search-institute.org/our-research/develop
ment-assets/developmental-assets-framework/

M. C. Black, K. C. Basile, M. J. Breidng, S. G. Smith, M. L.
Walters, M. T. Merrick, J. Chen, and M. R. Stevens. The
National Intimate Partner and Sexual Violence Survey
(NISVS), 2010 summary report, 2011. https://www.cdc
.gov/violenceprevention/datasources/nisvs/index.html.

Kay-Laurel Fischer and Mike McGrane. *Journey Beyond Abuse:
A Step-by-Step Guide to Facilitating Women's Domestic Abuse
Groups*. St. Paul, MN: Amherst H. Wilder Foundation,
1997. © Turner Publishing Company.

Kay-Laurel Fischer and Mike McGrane. *Moving Beyond Abuse: Stories and Questions for Women Who Have Lived with Abuse.* St. Paul, MN: Amherst H. Wilder Foundation, 1997. © Turner Publishing Company.

David J. Mathews. *Foundations for Violence-Free Living: A Step-by-Step Guide to Facilitating Men's Domestic Abuse Groups.* St. Paul, MN: Amherst H. Wilder Foundation, 1995. © Turner Publishing Company.

David J. Matthews. *On the Level: Foundations for Violence-Free Living.* St. Paul, MN: Amherst H. Wilder Foundation, 1995. © Turner Publishing Company.

Lenore E. Walker. *The Battered Woman.* New York: Harper Perennial, 1980.

ABOUT THE AUTHOR

In the early 1980s, Mike McGrane was the founder and director of one of the largest and most comprehensive domestic abuse counseling programs in the country. In three decades of facilitating treatment groups for perpetrators and victims/survivors, he developed an understanding and knowledge of the issues the program participants faced. He is the coauthor of a women's curriculum that describes a step-by-step treatment program for victims/survivors of domestic abuse.

Mike developed the treatment intervention tool known as *The House of Abuse* that has been replicated in numerous publications and is explained in great detail in this book. The stories and examples of its impact on treatment participants and general audiences will familiarize the reader with a tool that inspires discussion, understanding, and, in the best cases, changed behavior.

In addition to designing and implementing various prevention and intervention programs, Mike trained clinicians and audiences nationally and internationally. He worked with the Navy's Family Advocacy Program and other branches of the military to help develop domestic abuse programs.

Mike is a retired Navy officer with over twenty-five years

of active duty and reserve service. He also served on the board of directors and as chairperson for the first battered women's shelter in the country.

He has undergraduate and graduate degrees in social work and a minor in criminal justice studies from the University of Minnesota. Mike is a retired Licensed Independent Clinical Social Worker, MSW, LICSW. For thirteen years, he was community faculty, supervising social work graduate students and conducting field work seminars at the U of M.

In his retirement, he enjoys golfing and playing guitar in classic rock bands.